HOW TO COMMUNICATE WITH YOUR SPANISH SPEAKING HELP AND FRIENDS

"A Complete Spanish/English Guide"

The Housekeeper's Bible

(Spanish - *English* - **English Phonetics**)

La Biblia de La Empleada de Casa

(Español - *Inglés* - **Fonética en Inglés**)

1st printing, April 1989
2nd printing, June 1989
3rd printing, September 1989
4th printing, December 1989
5th printing, July 1991

Dedication

To my husband and my children for putting up with my hours of work getting this book together.

Thank you!

Liora

Dedicación

A mi esposo e hijos por aguantar las horas de trabajo para elaborar este libro.

¡Gracias!

Liora

Introducción

La comunicación siempre ha sido una prioridad para mi. Después de haber salido de la casa de mis padres en Caracas, Venezuela y haber llegado a los Estados Unidos y vivir por tantos años alrededor de gente que habla español e inglés. En muchas ocasiones me pedían que escribiera una guía/manual que fuera de uso doméstico/hogareño. Muy poco después de mi primera edición, como resultado de las increíbles respuestas que recibí por mi libro, me di cuenta que contenía toda la información necesaria para comunicarse en español e inglés para las "situaciones básicas diarias".

La "Biblia de la Empleada de Casa" ayudará a la comunicación entre amigos, empleados y *jefes*/patrones, pacientes y doctores, estudiantes y maestros, vecinos, clientes, padres, familias, viajeros, *etc., etc..* Es un libro muy personal donde le ayudará a crear su propia rutina de trabajo y ampliar las entrevistas necesarias. Las partes de conversación le dejará comunicarse efectivamente en español e inglés en cualquier situación.

Es importante recordar que algunas palabras en español se usan diferente en diferentes paises, ciudades, pueblos, etc. Cuando esto ocurra, por favor escriba al lado de la palabra el otro significado. (El uso de un diccionario puede ser de mayor ayuda.)

Un elemento esencial de este libro es la parte fonética, yo creo que va a ayudar muchísimo, aunque la pronunciación tal vez no sea perfecta ("la manera correcta") será suficiente para la ayuda de comunicación entre los de habla de español y de inglés.

Mantener este libro a la mano, donde ud. podrá leerlo en cualquier momento que lo necesite. Mi consejo es que se refiera a este libro todo el tiempo y así pronto aprenderá el idioma.

Este libro está escrito de la manera más sencilla que hasta un niño lo pueda utilizar.

Finalmente, por favor sea paciente. Toma tiempo para que alguien aprenda un idioma nuevo.

Buena Suerte!

Introduction
(Introdacshon)

Communication has always been a priority to me. After coming from my parents home in Caracas, Venezuela to the United States and living among Spanish and English speaking people here for many years, I was asked on many occasions to write a Spanish/English communication guide for household use. Shortly after the first printing and as a result of the incredible response I received for my book, I realized that it contains all the information needed to communicate in Spanish and English for "basic, everyday" situations.

"The Housekeeper's Bible" will help to ease communication between friends, employers-employees, patients-doctors, students-teachers, neighbors, clients, parents, families, travelers, etc., etc.

This is a personalized book allowing you to create your own schedule and even tailor your interviews to your needs.

The conversational sections will let you communicate effectively in Spanish or English in any situation.

It is important to remember that some Spanish words are used differently in different countries, cities, towns, etc. When this happens to you, please write the other meaning next to the word in question. (Using a dictionary might help.)

An essential element of the "The Housekeeper's Bible" is the phonetic sections. I believe they will be of considerable help. While the pronunciations may not be perfect ("the correct way"), they will be enough to help communications between Spanish and English speaking people.

Keep this book handy where you can read it anytime it is needed. My advice is to refer to this book at all times and soon anyone using it will be quickly learning the language.

This book is written in the simplest way so even a child can use it.

Finally, please be patient. It takes time for someone to learn a new language.

Good Luck!

Tabla de Contenido

Table of Contents

Cómo conseguir una empleada?
How to find a housekeeper
(Jau tu faind ei jauskiper)

1. Algunas estaciones de radio, donde hablan español, le pueden ayudar.
   Some radio stations where they speak Spanish can help you to find one.
2. Algunas iglesias de habla Hispánica le pueden ayudar.
   Some Spanish speaking churches can also help.
3. Por medio de una amiga que tenga una empleada, preguntarle a ella que si conoce a alguien que quiera trabajar.
   Ask your friend's housekeeper if she can help you to find one.
4. Poner un aviso en ambos periódicos : Español e Inglés.
   Place an ad in both newspapers : Spanish and English.
5. Llamar a una agencia de empleadas de casa.
   Call an agency for housekeepers.

Cómo conseguir trabajo?
How to find a job
(Jau tu faind ei yab)

1. Algunas estaciones de radio, donde hablan Español, le pueden ayudar.
   Some Spanish radio stations can help you find one.
2. Tu iglesia puede ayudarte.
   Your church can help you.
3. Lea los anuncios de trabajo en el periódico.
   Read the ads in the newspaper. Classified section.
4. Si tienes una amiga que trabaja en una casa que ella le pregunte a su jefa o patrona si no tiene amigas que ocupen empleadas.
   Ask your friends (if they work at a house) to ask their employers if they have friends that need a housekeeper.
5. Poner un anuncio en el periódico.
   Place an ad in the newspaper.
6. Llamar a una agencia de empleadas de casa.
   Call a housekeeper agency for a job.

Cómo leer español (Sonido fonético)?
How to read Spanish
(Jau tu rid spanish)

The vowels always have the same sound:

A   sounds like the "A" in CAT

E   sounds like the "E" in RED.

I   sounds like the "EE" as in BEEP.

O   sounds like the "O" in PORT.

U   sounds like the "U" in RULE.

The consonants that change from English to Spanish are:

C   sounds like **"S"** when it is followed by the vowels E and I; otherwise, it sounds like a normal **"C"**.

G   sounds like "H" in **HOUSE** when it is followed by the vowels "E" and "I"; otherwise, it sounds like the "G" in **GO**.

H   always silent

J   always sounds like the "H" in **HOUSE**>

LL   always sounds like the "Y" in **Y**OYO.

Ñ   always sounds like the "NY" in CA**NY**ON.

NOTE: For the word "you" in Spanish, "tu" or "Ud." is used. "Tu" is very informal and is the most frequently used. "Ud." is more formal and used to show respect, when speaking to someone not known well or to an older person. Throughout this book I have used both the formal and informal words to help you become familiar with both ways.

Palabras que ayudarán para la entrevista
Words that will help for the interview
(Wuords dat wil jelp for di interviu)

A mi manera:	My way: (Mai wuei)
Adiós:	Good bye: (Gud bai)
Ahora:	Now: (Nau)
Años:	Years: (Yirs)
Apellido:	Last Name: (Last Neim)
Aquí:	Here: (Jir)
Area código:	Area code: (Erea Coud)
Autobus/Camión:	Bus: (Bas)
Automático:	Automatic: (Otomatic)
Calle:	Street: (Strit)
Camión/Troca:	Truck: (Trak)
Carro:	Car: (Car)
Casado:	Married: (Merrid)
Cerca:	Near: (Nir)
Ciudad:	City: (Siti)
Claro:	Of course: (Of kors)
De acuerdo:	O.K: (Okei)
De cambio/Velocidades:	Standard: (Stenderd)
Diferente:	Different: (Diferent)
Divorciado:	Divorced: (Divors)
Día:	Day: (Dei)
Edad:	Age: (Eich)
Educación:	Education: (Edukeishon)
El:	He: (Ji)
Ella:	She: (Shi)
Entender/Comprender:	Understand: (Andersten)
Entrevista:	Interview: (interviu)
Estado:	State: (Esteit)
Estados Unidos:	U.S.A: (Yu-Es-Ei)
Fecha:	Date: (Deit)

Final:	End: **(End)**
Firma:	Signature: **(Signachur)**
Gracias:	Thank you: **(Ten kiu)**
Hacer:	Do: **(Du)**
Hoy:	Today: **(Tudei)**
Igual:	Same: **(Seim)**
Lejos:	Far. **(Far)**
Mañana:	Tomorrow: **(Tumorrou)**
Mes:	Month: **(Mans)**
Miedo:	Scared of: **(Skerd of)**
Mismo:	Same: **(Seim)**
Mío:	Mine: **(Main)**
Mucho:	Lot: **(Lat)**
Nada:	Nothing: **(Nasin)**
Necesito trabajar:	I need to work: **(Ai nid tu wuork)**
No estoy segura:	I am not sure: **(A yam nat shur)**
No lo sabía:	I did not Know: **(Ai did nat nou)**
No me gusta:	I don't like it: **(Ai dont laiket)**
No mucho:	Not much: **(Nat mach)**
No sé:	I don't know: **(Ai dont nou)**
No:	No: **(Nou)**
Nombre segundo (Medio):	Middle name: **(Midel neim)**
Nombre:	Name: **(Neim)**
Número:	Number. **(Namber)**
Otro:	Another: **(Enoder)**
Parte del tiempo:	Part time: **(Part taim)**
Poco:	Little: **(Litel)**
Por favor:	Please: **(Plis)**
Principio:	Beginning: **(Biginin)**
Problema:	Problem: **(Prablem)**
Pronto:	Soon: **(Sun)**
Puedo:	Can: **(Ken)**
Quizás:	Maybe: **(Meibi)**
Rápido:	Fast: **(Fast)**
Seguro:	Sure: **(Shur)**

Separado:	*Separated: **(Separeited)***
Si me gusta:	*I like it: **(Ai laiket)***
Si:	*Yes: **(Lies)***
Soltero:	*Single: **(Singel)***
Sólo/solamente:	*Only: **(Onli)***
Suficiente:	*Enough: **(Enof)***
Suyo:	*Theirs: **(Ders)***
Tal vez:	*Maybe: **(Meibi)***
Talla:	*Size: **(Sais)***
Temporal/Temporario:	*Temporary: **(Temporeri)***
Tengo:	*Have: **(Jev)***
Tiempo completo:	*Full time: **(Ful taim)***
Tu/Ud:	*You: **(Yu)***
Tuyo:	*Yours: **(Yors)***
Viudo(a):	*Widow/Widower.*
	(Wuidou/Wuidower)
Yo creo:	*I think so: **(Ai sink sou)***
Yo quiero aprender:	*I want to learn: **(Ai wuant tu lern)***
Yo quiero:	*I want: **(Ai wuant)***
Yo:	*I **(Ai)***
Zona postal:	*Zip code: **(Zip Coud)***

Words that will help for the interview
(Wuords dat wil jelp for di interviu)
Palabras que ayudarán para la entrevista

Age: *(Eich)*	Edad:
Another: *(Enoder)*	Otro:
Area code: *(Erea Coud)*	Area código:
Automatic: *(Otomatic)*	Automático:
Beginning: *(Biginin)*	Principio:
Bus: *(Bas)*	Autobus/Camión:
Can: *(Ken)*	Puedo:
Car: *(Car)*	Carro:
City: *(Siti)*	Ciudad:
Date: *(Deit)*	Fecha:
Day: *(Dei)*	Día:
Different: *(Diferent)*	Diferente:
Divorced: *(Divors)*	Divorciado:
Do: *(Du)*	Hacer:
Education: *(Edukeishon)*	Educación:
End: *(End)*	Final:
Enough: *(Enof)*	Suficiente:
Far: *(Far)*	Lejos:
Fast: *(Fast)*	Rápido:
Full time: *(Ful taim)*	Tiempo completo:
Good bye: *(Gud bai)*	Adiós:
Have: *(Jev)*	Tengo:
He: *(Ji)*	El:
Here: *(Jir)*	Aquí:
I am not sure: *(A yam nat shur)*	No estoy segura:
I did not know: *(Al did nat nou)*	No lo sabía:
I don't know: *(Al dont nou)*	No sé:
I don't like it: *(Al dont laiket)*	No me gusta:
I like it: *(Al laiket)*	Si me gusta:

I need to work: *(Ai nid tu wuork)*	Necesito trabajar:
I think so: *(Ai sink sou)*	Yo creo:
I want to learn: *(Ai wuant tu lern)*	Yo quiero aprender:
I want: *(Ai wuant)*	Yo quiero:
I: *(Ai)*	Yo:
Interview: *(interviu)*	Entrevista:
Last Name: *(Last Neim)*	Apellido:
Little: *(Litel)*	Poco:
Lot: *(Lat)*	Mucho:
Married: *(Merrid)*	Casado:
Maybe: *(Meibi)*	Quizás:
Maybe: *(Meibi)*	Tal vez:
Middle name: *(Midel neim)*	Nombre segundo (Medio):
Mine: *(Main)*	Mío:
Month: *(Mans)*	Mes:
My way: *(Mai wuei)*	A mi manera:
Name: *(Neim)*	Nombre:
Near: *(Nir)*	Cerca:
No: *(Nou)*	No:
Not much: *(Nat mach)*	No mucho:
Nothing: *(Nasin)*	Nada:
Now: *(Nau)*	Ahora:
Number: *(Namber)*	Número:
O.K: *(Okei)*	De acuerdo:
Of course: *(Of kors)*	Claro:
Only: *(Onli)*	Sólo/solamente:
Part time: *(Part taim)*	Parte del tiempo:
Please: *(Plis)*	Por favor:
Problem: *(Prablem)*	Problema:
Same: *(Seim)*	Igual:
Same: *(Seim)*	Mismo:
Scared of: *(Skerd of)*	Miedo:
Separated: *(Separeited)*	Separado:

She: *(Shi)*	Ella:
Signature: *(Signachur)*	Firma:
Single: *(Singel)*	Soltero:
Size: *(Sais)*	Talla:
Soon: *(Sun)*	Pronto:
Standard: *(Stenderd)*	De Cambio/Velocidades:
State: *(Esteit)*	Estado:
Street: *(Strit)*	Calle:
Sure: *(Shur)*	Seguro:
Temporary: *(Temporeri)*	Temporal/Temporario:
Thank you: *(Ten kiu)*	Gracias:
Theirs: *(Ders)*	Suyo:
Today: *(Tudei)*	Hoy:
Tomorrow: *(Tumorrou)*	Mañana:
Truck: *(Trak)*	Camión/Troca:
U.S.A: *(Yu-Es-Ei)*	Estados Unidos:
Understand: *(Andersten)*	Entender/Comprender:
Widow/Widower: *(Wuidou/Wuidower)*	Viudo(a):
Years: *(Yirs)*	Años:
Yes: *(Lles)*	Si:
You: *(Yu)*	Tu/Ud:
Yours: *(Yors)*	Tuyo:
Zip code: *(Zip Coud)*	Zona postal:

Cómo entrevistar a una empleada?
How to interview a housekeeper
(Jau to interviu ei jauskiper)

1. Hablas y entiendes inglés?
   Do you speak and understand English?
   (Du yu spik and andersten inglish?)

2. Cómo te llamas?
   What is your name?
   (Wuat is yor neim?)

3. Cuántos años tienes?
   How old are you?
   (Jau old ar yu?)

4. Eres legal?
   Are you legal?
   (Ar yu ligal)

5. Tienes papeles de imigración?
   Do you have any papers of immigration?
   (Du yu jev eni peipers of imigreshon?)

6. Cuánto tiempo tienes en U.S.A?
   How long have you been here in the U.S.A?
   (Jau long jev yu bin jir in di U.S.A?)

7. De dónde eres (qué país)?
   Where are you from? (which country)?
   (Wuer ar yu from? (wuich kantri)?)

8. Quieres trabajar en casa?
   Do you want to work at home?
   (Du yu wuant to wuork at jom?)

9. Sabes leer y escribir?
   Do you know how to read and write?
   (Du yu nou jau tu rid en rait?)

10. En inglés, también?
    In English too?
    (In inglish tu?)

11. Dónde vives (ahora)?
    Where do you live (now)?
    (Wuer du yu liv (Nau)?)

12. Tienes teléfono?
    Do you have a phone number?
    (Du yu jev ei fon namber?)

13. Estás soltera o casada?
    Are you single or married?
    (Ar yu singel o merrid?)

14. Tienes hijos? Cuántos?
    Do you have any children? How many?
    (Du yu jev ení children? Jau Meni?)

15. Tienes quién te traiga y te lleve?
    Do you have a ride from and to work?
    (Du yu jev ei raid from en tu wuork?)

16. Tienes familia aquí?
    Do you have family here?
    (Du yu jev femili jir?)

17. Tu manejas?
    Do you drive?
    (Du yu draiv?)

18. Tienes carro?
    Do you have a car?
    (Du yu jev ei kar?)

19. Has trabajado antes en casa?
    Have you ever worked in a house before?
    (Jev yu ever wuork in ei jaus bifor?)

20. Tu fumas?
    Do you smoke?
    (Du yu smouk?)

21. Cuánto tiempo piensas quedarte aquí en los U.S.A.?
    How long are you planning to stay in the U.S.A.?
    (Jau long ar yu plenin tu stei in di U.S.A.?)

11

22. Tienes licencia de manejar?
Do you have a driver's license?
(Du yu jev ei draivers laisens?)

23. Sabes cuidar niños?
Do you know how to take care of children?
(Du yu nou jau tu teik ker of children?)

24. Infante/recién nacido o bebé?
An infant or a baby?
(En infant or ei beibi?)

25. Sabes bañar y alimentar a un bebé?
Do you know how to bathe or feed a baby?
(Du yu nou jau tu beis or fid ei beibi?)

26. Te gustan los niños y bebés?
Do you like children and babies?
(Du yu laik children end beibis?)

27. Te gustan los animales?
Do you like animals?
(Du yu laik enimals?)

28. Sabes cómo cuidarlos?
Do you know how to take care of them?
(Du yu nou jau tu teik ker of em?)

29. Sabes cómo atender el teléfono?
Do you know how to answer the telephone?
(Du yu nou jau tu enser di telefon?)

30. Sabes cómo usar artefáctos eléctricos?
Do you know how to use electric appliances?
(Du yu nou jau tu llus electric aplaienses?)

31. Sabes planchar?
Do you know how to iron?
(Du yu nou jau tu airon?)

32. Sabes cocinar?
Do you know how to cook?
(Du yu nou jau tu kuk?)

33. Cuántos días quieres trabajar?
How many days do you want to work?
(Jau meni deis du yu wuant tu wuork?)

34. Cuánto quieres ganar?
How much money do you want to be paid?
(Jau mach mani du yu wuant tu bi peid?)

35. Tiene tarjeta del seguro social?
Do you have a social security card?
(Du yu jev ei soshial sekiuriti kard?)

36. Tienes uniformes?
Do you have any uniforms?
(Du yu jev eni yuniforms?)

37. Sabes coser?
Do you know how to sew?
(Du yu nou jau tu sou?)

38. Cuándo quieres empezar a trabajar?
When do you want to start to work?
(Wuen du yu guant tu start tu wuork?)

39. Tienes referencias?
Do you have any references?
(Du yu jev eni referenses?)

40. Tiene alguna enfermedad contagiosa?
Do you have any contagious sickness?
(Du yu jev eni conteillios siknes?)

41. Tienes seguro médico - (aseguranza)?
Do you have medical insurance?
(Du yu jev medikol inshurans?)

42. Me das tu número de teléfono y tu dirección?
Can you give me your phone number and your address?
(Ken yu giv mi yor fon namber end yor adres?)

43. Yo quiero que trabajes con nosotros.
I want you to work for us.
(Ai want yu tu wourk for as.)

44. Empiezas_____.
    You will start_____.
    (Yu wil start_____.)

45. Voy a pensarlo y te aviso.
    I'm going to think about it and I will let you know.
    (Ayam goin tu sink about it end ai wil let yu nou.)

46. Le tengo que hablar a mi esposo(a).
    I have to talk to my husband - wife (spouse)..
    (Ai jev tu tok tu mai jasband - wuaif (spaus).)

47. No estoy interesada, gracias.
    I'm not interested, thank you.
    (Ayam nat interested tenkiu.)

48. Estás interesada en el trabajo?
    Are you interested in the job?
    (Ar yu interested in di llab?)

49. Estás dispuesta a trabajar en lo que sea?
    Are you willing to work in any job?
    (Ar yu wilin tu wuork in eni yab?)

50. Ha tenido algún problema con la ley?
    Have you ever had a problem with the law?
    (Jev yu ever jed el prablem wis di lo?)

51. Si Sí, qué y cuándo?
    If yes, what and when?
    (If lles, wuat end wuen?)

52. Quiere trabajar para dormir adentro o para trabajar de entrada por salida?
    Do you want to be a live-in or day help?
    (Du yu wuant tu bi el livin or dei jelp?)

Horario
Time set up
(Taim set ap)

Día de entrada:
Day in:
(Dei in):

Hora de entrada:
Time in:
(Taim in):

Día de sálida:
Day out:
(Dei aut):

Hora de sálida:
Time out:
(Taim aut):

Día(s) libre:
Day(s) off:
(Dei(s) off):

Mascotas: Animales
Pets: Animals
(Pets: Énimols)

Acuario:	Fish tank: *(Fish tenk)*
Ardilla:	Squirrel: *(Skuerl)*
Caballo:	Horse: *(Jors)*
Cochino/Cerdo:	Pig: *(Pig)*
Cocodrillo/Caimán:	Alligator: *(Alegeitor)*
Culebra:	Snake: *(Sneik)*
Elefante:	Elephant: *(Élefant)*
Gato:	Cat: *(Kat)*
Jaula:	Cage: *(Keich)*
Jemster:	Hamster: *(Jemster)*
Jirafa:	Giraffe: *(Yiraf)*
León:	Lion: *(Laion)*
Lobo:	Wolf: *(Wuolf)*
Mono/Chango:	Monkey: *(Manki)*
Oso:	Bear: *(Ber)*
Oveja:	Sheep: *(Ship)*
Pájaro:	Bird: *(Berd)*
Perro:	Dog: *(Dog)*
Pez:	Fish: *(Fish)*
Rata:	Rat: *(Rat)*
Ratón:	Mouse: *(Maus)*
Tigre:	Tiger: *(taiger)*
Tortuga:	Turtle: *(Tertel)*
Zorro:	Fox: *(Fax)*

.

Pets: Animals
(Pets: Énimols)
Mascotas: Animales

Alligator: *(Alegeitor)*	Cocodrillo/Caimán:
Bear: *(Ber)*	Oso:
Bird: *(Berd)*	Pájaro:
Cage: *(Keich)*	Jaula:
Cat: *(Kat)*	Gato:
Dog: *(Dog)*	Perro:
Elephant: *(Élefant)*	Elefante:
Fish: *(Fish)*	Pez:
Fish Tank: *(Fish tenk)*	Acuario:
Fox: *(Fax)*	Zorro:
Giraffe: *(Yiraf)*	Jirafa:
Hamster: *(Jemster)*	Jemster:
Horse: *(Jors)*	Caballo:
Lion: *(Laion)*	León:
Monkey: *(Manki)*	Mono/Chango:
Mouse: *(Maus)*	Ratón:
Pig: *(Pig)*	Cochino/Cerdo:
Rat: *(Rat)*	Rata:
Sheep: *(Ship)*	Oveja:
Snake: *(Sneik)*	Culebra:
Squirrel: *(Skuerl)*	Ardilla:
Tiger: *(taiger)*	Tigre:
Turtle: *(Tertel)*	Tortuga:
Wolf: *(Wuolf)*	Lobo:

Cuestionario para rutina del trabajo
Questionnaire for work routine
(Kuestioner for wuork rutin)

Rellenar este cuestionario para ayudarle planear la rutina diaria del trabajo de casa que ud. quiere que se haga y luego escribir su horario que está en las páginas siguientes:

Fill out this questionnaire to help you set up the routine of the housework you want done and then make your own schedule using the following pages:

Usar las siguientes respuestas
Use the following answers
(Yus di falowin ensers)

D:	Diario:	*Daily: (Deili)*
M:	Lunes:	*Monday: (Mandei)*
Tu:	Martes:	*Tuesday: (Tusdei)*
W:	Miércoles:	*Wednesday: (Wensdei)*
Th:	Jueves:	*Thursday: (Sursdei)*
F:	Viernes:	*Friday: (Fraidei)*
Sat:	Sábado:	*Saturday: (Saturdei)*
Sun:	Domingo:	*Sunday: (Sandei)*
1/M:	Una vez al mes:	*Once a month: (Wans el mons)*
2/M:	Dos veces al mes:	*Twice a month: (Tuals e mons)*
E/W:	Una vez cada dos semanas:	*Every other week: (Evri ader wlk)*
E/M:	Una vez cada dos meses:	*Every other month: (Evri ader mons)*
N/A:	No aplicable:	*Not applicable: (Nat aplicabol)*
W/N:	Cuando sea necesario:	*When needed: (Wuen nided)*

Para algunas labores incluir la hora.
For some chores include time

Despertarse: *Wake up: (Weikap)* _____

Estar en la cocina: *Be in the kitchen: (Bi in di kitchen)* _____

Despertar (Niños, señores):   *Wake up (Kids, Mr./Mrs.): (Weikap/Kids - mister - mises)* _____

Hacer el desayuno: *Make breakfast: (Meik Brekfast)* _____

Cambiar las sábanas: *Change the sheets: (Cheinch di shits)* _____

Sacudir/Limpiar el polvo de los dormitorios/recámaras:
                            Wipe/dust bedrooms: (Waip/dast bedrums) _____

Sacudir/Limpiar el polvo de la sala de visitas:
                            Wipe/dust the living room: (Waip/dast di livin rum) _____

Sacudir/Limpiar el polvo de la sala de familia:
                            Wipe/dust the family room: (Waip/dast di femili rum) _____

Sacudir/Limpiar el polvo del comedor: *Wipe/dust the dining room: (Waip/dast di dainin rum)* _____

Sacudir/Limpiar el polvo del cuarto de visita:
                            Wipe/dust the guest room: (Waip/dast di ges rum) _____

Sacudir/Limpiar el polvo de _____ :
                            Wipe/dust the _____ : (Waip/dast di _____) _____

Limpiar los baños:

Clean the bathrooms: (*Clin di basrums*) _____

Hacer las camas:

Make the beds: (*Meik di beds*)

_____

Lavar y secar ropa:

Wash and dry clothes: (*Wash end drai clous*) _____

Lavar a mano ropa:

Wash clothes by hand: (*Wuash clous bai jend*) _____

Planchar ropa:

Iron/press clothes: (*Airon/pres clous*) _____

Aspirar la casa:

Run vacuum all over the house: (*Ran vakium ol over di jaus*)

_____

Lavar adentro de la nevera/refrigerador:

Clean the inside of the refrigerator: (*Clin di insaid of di rifrillireitor*) _____

Limpiar adentro del horno:

Clean the inside of the oven: (*Clin di insaid of di aven*)

_____

Limpiar el micro-ondas:

Clean the microwave: (*Clin di maicroweiv*) _____

Limpiar el congelador/friser:

Clean the freezer: (*Clin di friser*)

_____

Limpiar a fondo la estufa:

Clean the stove: (*Clin di stoub*)

_____

Barrer el piso:

Sweep the floor: (*Suip di flor*)

_____

Trapear el piso:

Mop the floor: (*Map di flor*)

_____

Barrer afuera:

Sweep outside: (*Suip Autsaid*)

_____

Limpiar los muebles de afuera:

Clean the patio furniture: (*Clin di patio furnichur*) _____

Sacudir/Quitar polvo de los sofás: *Fluff sofas: **(Flaf soufas)***

_____

Cambiar toallas: *Change towels: **(Cheinch***
*   **taguels)** _____*

Arreglar y limpiar los dormitorios/recámaras:
Straighten and clean up the
*bedrooms: **(Streiten en clin ap***
* **di bedrums)** _____*

Arreglar y limpiar la sala de familia: *Straighten and clean up the family*
*room: **(Streiten en clin ap de***
* **femili rum)** _____*

Arreglar y limpiar la sala de visitas: *Straighten and clean up the living*
*room: **(Streiten en clin ap di***
* **livin rum)** _____*

Arreglar y limpiar el comedor: *Straighten and clean up the dining*
*room: **(Streiten en clin di***
* **dainin rum)** _____*

Arreglar y limpiar la cocina: *Straighten and clean up the*
*kitchen: **(Streiten end clin ap***
* **di kitchen.)** _____*

Arreglar y limpiar el cuarto de juegos:
Straighten and clean up the game
*room: **(Streiten end clin ap***
* **geim rum)** _____*

Arreglar y limpiar el lavadero/cuarto de lavar:
Straighten and clean up the laundry
*room: **(Streiten and clin ap di***
* **laundri rum)** _____*

Otro _____ :   *Other: **(Ader)**_____*

Arreglar y limpiar el garaje: *Straighten and clean up the*
*garage: **(Streiten and clin ap di***
* **garach)** _____*

Barrer el garaje: *Sweep the garage: **(Suip di***
* **garach)** _____*

Recoger la basura de los basureros en todos los cuartos:

*Collect the garbage from all the rooms: (**Colect di garbich from ol di rums**)* _____

Poner la basura afuera:

*Take the garbage outside: (**Teik di garbich autsaid**)* _____

Limpiar las ventanas:

*Clean the windows: (**Clin di windous**)* _____

Limpiar las persianas:

*Clean the blinds: (**Clin di blainds**)* _____

Pasarle aceite a los muebles de madera y todo lo que tiene madera:

*Oil the wood furniture and wood work: (**Oil di wud wourk end wud furnichur**)* _____

Arreglar los closets:

*Straighten up the closets: (**Streiten ap di closets**)*

_____

Regar las plantas:

*Water the plants: (**Guater di plents**)* _____

Pulir la platería:

*Polish the silver: (**Polish di silver**)* _____

Poner la mesa:

*Set the table: (**Set di teibol**)*

_____

Recoger el correo:

*Pick up the mail: (**Pik ap di meil**)*

_____

Recoger el periódico afuera:

*Bring in the newspaper (outside): (**Bring in di niuspeiper - autsaid**)* _____

Poner la ropa sucia en el ropero (cesta):

*Put the dirty clothes in the hamper: (**Put di derti clous in di jemper**)* _____

Encerar el piso:

*Wax the floors: (**Wuax di flors**)*

_____

Otras Cosas: *Other: (Ader)*

Si tiene niños
If you have children
(If yu jev children)

Despertarlos:

Wake them up: *(Weik dem ap)*
_____

Desayuno:

Breakfast: *(Brekfast)*
_____

Alimentar al bebé:

Feed baby at: *(Fid beibi at)*
_____

Hora de bañar:

Bathing time: *(Beidin taim)*
_____

Hacer almuerzo/lonche:

Make lunch: *(Meik lanch)*
_____

Hacer almuerzo/lonchera para el colegio/escuela:

Make lunch for school: *(Meik lanch for skul)* _____

Preparar niños para el colegio/escuela:

Get the children ready for school: *(Get di children redi for skul)*
_____

Hora que vienen por ellos:

Car pool time: *(Car pul taim)*
_____

Vaya con ellos hasta el carro:

Go with them to the car. *(Gou wis dem tu de car)* _YES OR NO_

Siesta:

Nap time: *(Nap time)*
_____

Hora de Merienda:

Time for snacks: *(Taim for snaks)* _____

Tarea:

Homework: *(Jomwuork)*
_____

Ir afuera a jugar:

Go outside to play: *(Go autsaid to plei)* _____

Con ellos:

With them: *(wis dem)* _YES OR NO_

Hora de jugar:	*Playtime: **(Pleitaim)*** _____
Hora de cenar:	*Dinner time: **(Diner taim)***
	_____
Hora de dormir:	*Bedtime: **(Bedtaim)*** _____
Hora de regreso del colegio/escuela:	
	Time back from school or other:
	(Taim bak from skul)
	_____
Nombres:	*Names: **(Neims)*** _____
Edades:	*Ages: **(Ailles)*** _____
Otras cosas:	*Other: **(Ader)*** _____

Si tiene una mascota (animal):
If you have a pet:
(If yu jev ei pet):

Tipo de mascota:

Type of pet: (Taip of pet)

_____

Nombre:

Name: (Neim) _____

Sexo:

Sex: (Sex) _____

Hora de comer:

Feeding time: (Fidin taim)

_____

Cambiar el agua:

Change the water: (Cheinch di water) _____

Bañar:

Bathe: (Beid) _____

Dejarlo Salir:

Time out: (Taim aut)

_____

Dejarlo Entrar:

Time in: (Taim in)

_____

Otras cosas:

Other: (Ader) _____

Qué hacer todos los días?
What to do everyday
(Wuat tu du evridei)

Qué hacer todos los días?
What to do everyday
(Wuat tu du evridei)

Extras

Lunes: *Monday: (**Mandei**)*

Martes: *Tuesday: (**Tusdei**)*

Miércoles: *Wednesday: **(Wensdei)***

Jueves: *Thursday: **(Sursdei)***

Viernes: Friday: *(Fraidei)*

Sábado: Saturday: *(Saturdei)*

Domingo: Sunday: *(Sandei)*

Una vez cada   *Every other week:*
dos semanas: *(Evri ader wik)*

Una vez al mes: *Once a month:*
                                                     (Uans e mons)

Una vez cada dos meses: *Every other month:*
                                                     (Evri ader mans)

33

Horario de los niños:
Schedule for the children:
(Skedyul for kids:)

Horario para la mascota de la casa:
Schedule for the pet of the house:
(Skedyul for di pet of di jaus)

Lista de cosas de limpiar
List of cleaning supplies
(List of clinin soplais)

Make sure to have all these items before you start a new housekeeper in your home.

Aceite para muebles de madera: Oil cleaner for wood furniture: *(Oil cliner for wud furnichur)*

Almidón: Starch: *(Starch)*

Amonía: Ammonia: *(Emonia)*

Aspiradora: Vacuum cleaner. *(Vakium cliner)*

Bolsas de aspiradora: Vacuum bag: *(Vakium bag)*

Bolsas de basura: Garbage bags: *(Garbich bags)*

Brillo: Brillo Pads: *(Brilo Peds)*

Cepillo para el excusado: Toilet brush: *(Tuolet brash)*

Cepillo: Scrub brush: *(Scrab brash)*

Cera: Wax: *(Wuax)*

Cloro: Clorox, Bleach: *(Clorax, Blich)*

Crema para lustrar bronce: Brass polish: *(Bras polish)*

Crema para lustrar platería: Silver polish: *(Silver polish)*

Cubeta/Tobo: Pail/bucket: *(Peil/baket)*

Desinfectante: Disinfectant: *(Desinfectant)*

Detergente Líquido para lavar platos a mano: Liquid detergent to wash dishes by hand: *(Likuid detergent to wash dished bai jend)*

Detergente para lavaplatos: Dishwasher detergent: *(Dishwasher deterllent)*

Detergente para la ropa: Clothes detergent: *(Clous deterllent)*

Escoba: Broom: *(Brum)*

Esponja: Sponge: *(Sponch)*

Esprei para limpiar la alfombra:	*Spray cleaner for carpets*: **(Sprei cliner for carpets)**
Filtro:	*Filter*: **(Filter)**
Jabón líquido para ropa delicada:	*Liquid soap for hand washing (delicate) clothes*: **(Likuid soup for jend washin (delikeit) clous)**
Jabón:	*Soap*: **(Soup)**
Limpiador de horno:	*Oven cleaner*: **(Aven cliner)**
Líquido para limpiar el moho:	*Mildew cleaner*: **(Meldiu cliner)**
Líquido para limpiar vidrio, espejos, cromo, acero	
	Liquid to clean glass, mirror chrome, steel: **(Likuid tu clin glas - mirror - crom - stil)**
Mapeador/trapeador:	*Mop*: **(Map)**
Pala de recoger basura:	*Dust pan*: **(Dast pen)**
Para la secadora (Suavizador):	*Fabric softener*: **(Fabric softener)**
Polvo para limpiar:	*Cleanser (powder)*: **(Clinser pauder)**
Quita manchas:	*Spot cleaner*: **(Spat cliner)**
Toalla de papel:	*Paper towel*: **(Peiper tawel)**
Toallas:	*Towel*: **(Tawel)**
Trapo/paño:	*Rag*: **(Rag)**

List of cleaning supplies
(List of clinin soplais)
Lista de cosas de limpiar

Make sure to have all these items before you start a new housekeeper in your home.

Ammonia: *(Emonia)*	Amonía:
Brass polish: *(Bras polish)*	Crema para lustrar bronce:
Brillo Pads: *(Brilo Peds)*	Brillo:
Broom: *(Brum)*	Escoba:
Cleanser (powder): *(Clinser pauder)*	
	Polvo para limpiar:
Clorox, Bleach: *(Clorax, Blich)*	Cloro:
Clothes detergent: *(Clous deterllent)*	
	Detergente para la ropa:
Dishwasher detergent: *(Dishwasher deterllent)*	
	Detergente para lavaplatos:
Disinfectant: *(Desinfectant)*	Desinfectante:
Dust pan: *(Dast pen)*	Pala de recoger basura:
Fabric softener: *(Fabric softener)* .	
	Para la secadora (Suavizador):
Filter: *(Filter)*	Filtro:
Garbage bags: *(Garbich bags)*	Bolsas de basura:

Liquid detergent to wash dishes by hand *(Likuid detergent to wash dished bai jend)*

Detergente Líquido para lavar platos a mano:

Liquid soap for hand washing (delicate) clothes *(Likuid soup for jend washin (delikeit) clous)*

Jabón líquido para ropa delicada:

*Liquid to clean glass, mirror chrome, steel (**Likuid tu clin***

glas - mirror - crom - stil)   Líquido para limpiar vidrio, espejos,

                                   cromo, acero:

*Mildew cleaner: (**Meldiu cliner**)* Líquido para limpiar el moho:

*Mop: (**Map**)*   Mapeador/trapeador:

*Oil cleaner for wood furniture: (**Oil cliner for wud furnichur**)*

                                   Aceite para muebles de madera:

*Oven cleaner: (**Aven cliner**)*   Limpiador de horno:

*Pail/bucket: (**Peil/baket**)*   Cubeta/Tobo:

*Paper towel: (**Peiper tawel**)*   Toalla de papel:

*Rag: (**Rag**)*   Trapo/paño:

*Scrub brush: (**Scrab brash**)*   Cepillo:

*Silver polish: (**Silver polish**)*   Crema para lustrar platería:

*Soap: (**Soup**)*   Jabón:

*Sponge: (**Sponch**)*   Esponja:

*Spot cleaner: (**Spat cliner**)*   Quita manchas:

*Spray cleaner for carpets: (**Sprei cliner for carpets**)*

                                   Esprei para limpiar la alfombra:

*Starch: (**Starch**)*   Almidón:

*Toilet brush: (**Tuolet brash**)*   Cepillo para el excusado:

*Towel: (**Tawel**)*   Toallas:

*Vacuum bag: (**Vakium bag**)*   Bolsas de aspiradora:

*Vacuum cleaner: (**Vakium cliner**)*

                                   Aspiradora:

*Wax: (**Wuax**)*   Cera:

Marcas de productos de limpieza que Ud. usa
Name brand of cleaning supplies that you use

Polvo de limpiar: *Cleanser (powder):_____*

Detergente de ropa: *Clothes detergent:_____*

Detergente para lavaplatos: *Dishwater detergent:_____*

Detergente líquido para lavar platos a mano:

                                  Liquid detergent to wash dishes by hand: _____

Jabón: *Soap: _____*

Jabón Líquido para ropa delicada: *Liquid soap for hand washing delicate clothes:_____*

Cera: *Wax: _____*

Aceite para madera: *Oil cleaner: _____*

Almidón: *Starch: _____*

Cloro: *Clorox - bleach: _____*

Bolsa de aspiradora: *Vacuum bag:_____*

Líquido para limpiar vidrio, espejo, etc:

                                  Liquid to clean glass, mirror, etc:_____

Crema para lustrar platería: *Silver polish:_____*

Crema para lustrar bronce: *Brass polish:_____*

Líquido para limpiar el moho: *Mildew cleaner:_____*

Desinfectante: *Disinfectant:_____*

Esprei para limpiar la alfombra: *Spray cleaner for carpets:_____*

Suavizador para la secadora: *Fabric softener:_____*

Quita manchas: *Spot cleaner:_____*

Brillo (esponjas metálicas):   *Scrubbing pads:_____*

Amonía: *Ammonia:_____*

Limpiador de horno: *Oven cleaner:_____*

Información Vital
Vital Information

Name: **(Neim)**   Nombre:

_____

Telephone #: **(Telefon)**   Teléfono

_____

Address: **(Adres)**   Dirección:

_____

Kids: **(Children - kids)**   Niños:

_____

_____

Pet: **(Pet)**   Mascota:

_____

Emergency #: **(Emerllensi)**   Emergencia:
Police: **(Polis)**   Policía:
Ambulance: **(Embiulens)**   Ambulancia:
Fire Department: Bomberos:
(Faier Department)
Doctor: **(Dactor)**   Doctor:
Doctor: **(Dactor)**   Doctor:

(Better to use a pencil for any changes)
Usar la página siguiente para números adicionales.
Use the following page for extra numbers.

Reglas:
Rules:
(Ruls:)

Some of these rules may not apply to your household, so just cross them out. Thanks!

1. *Do not open the door for strangers.*
___ No abrir la puerta a personas extrañas.
2. *Make sure that all appliances are turned "OFF" after use. (Including: stove - oven - iron - toaster etc.)*
___ Asegurarse de apagar (OFF) todos los artefactos eléctricos después de usarlos. (Incluyendo: horno - hornillas - plancha - tostadora etc.)
3. *Do not leave any doors open, unlocked or the garage open.*
___ No dejar las puertas abiertas o sin llave - o el garaje abierto.
4. *Take care of everything in the house like it is your own. Try not to break anything.*
___ Cuidar todas las cosas en la casa como si fuera de uno, tratar de no romper nada.
5. *Do not abuse the use of the telephone, make short calls. Make sure not to get any calls before _____ AM or after _____ PM. Do not make long distance calls.*
___ No abusar del uso del teléfono, hacer llamadas breves. No recibir llamas antes de las _____ AM o después de las _____ PM. No hacer llamadas de larga distancia.
6. *No smoking, no drinking and no visitors.*
Comments:

___ No fumar, no beber y no visitas.
"Comentarios:

7. *Do not take anything with out asking for permission first.*

___ No tomar/agarrar algo ajeno sin primero preguntar por ello o permiso.

8. *Take a shower every day, use deodorant and look presentable at all times.*

___ Bañarse todos los días, usar desodorante y verse presentable/ordenado de apariencias todo el tiempo.

9. *Talk with respect at all times.*

___ Hablar con respeto todo el tiempo.

10. *Be honest, always tell the truth.*

___ Ser honesto y decir siempre la verdad.

11. *Do not leave any lights on, save electricity.*

___ No dejar ninguna luz encendida, hay que conservar electricidad.

12. *Write down all messages please.*

___ Por favor escribir todos los mensajes.

13. *Wash your hands before preparing any food.*

___ Lavarse las manos antes be preparar cualquier comida.

14. *Keep all medicines and cleaning supplies out of the reach of children or pets.*

___ Mantener todas las medicinas, productos de limpieza fuera del alcance de los niños o mascotas.

15. *Do not flush tampons, sanitary towels, hair or anything other than toilet paper.*

___ No bajar en el excusado tapones, toallas sanitarias, pelo u otro objeto que no sea papel sanitario (tualet).

16. *Always read clothing labels carefully, if it says: dry clean only :do not wash at home.*

___ Siempre ver las etiquetas de la ropa, si dice: dry clean only: no lavar en la casa.

17. *Always check the date on dairy products.*

___ Siempre ver la fecha de los productos lácteos.

18. *Please wash all vegetables and fruits before eating them.*

___ Por favor lavar todos los vegetales y frutas antes de comer.

19. *Keep refrigerator and freezer doors closed.*

___ Mantenga las puertas de la nevera/refrigeradora y del frizer cerradas.

20. *Do not leave babies or children unattended when they are in the bathtub.*

___ Ne deje sin atender a los bebés o niños cuando estan en la bañera/tina.

21. *When anything glass breaks, pick up the pieces carefully and quickly.*

___ Si algo the vidrio se rompe recogerlo con cuidado y rápido (todos los pedazos).

22. *Do not leave small children playing outside by themselves.*

___ No dejar niños pequeños sólos cuando están jugando afuera.

23. *In case of fire get everyone (even pets) outside of the house.*

___ En caso de fuego sacar a todos afuera de la casa (incluyendo a la mascota).

24. *In case of any emergency or accident call me, or call the ambulance or _____.*

___ En caso de una emergencia o accidente llamarme, o a la ambulancia o _____.

Here is some space for you to write more rules:

46

Tips:
(Tips)
Consejos:

1. *Use hot water when washing dishes by hand.*
   ___ Usar agua caliente cuando laven a mano los platos.
2. *Do not use any metal dishes- utensils- wires- twisters- foil in the microwave.*
   ___ No usar en el micro-ondas nada que sea de metal o papel aluminio- twisters- alambres- utensilios de cocina de metal.
3. *Do not put any bones- grease- seeds- trash (paper- rubber- metal) into the disposal.*
   ___ No poner huesos- grasa (aceite)- semillas- basura (papel- plástico- metal) adentro del desechador.
4. *While cleaning the house, run the washer and dryer to save some worktime.*
   ___ Mientras uno limpia la casa, lavar y secar ropa para ahorrar tiempo de trabajo.
5. *When using the disposal, run cold water.*
   ___ Cuando use el desechador de comida correr agua fría.
6. *When something spills on furniture, fabric, or carpet wipe it off with cold water.*
   ___ Cuando algo se derrame encima de los muebles, telas, alfombras, límpielo rápido con agua fría.
7. *When a child or baby gets soap or shampoo in their eyes, rinse them with water.*
   ___ Si le entra jabón o shampú al niño o bebé en los ojos enjuague con agua.
8. *Do not wash bright colors with light colors.*
   ___ No lavar colores vivos con colores claros.

9. *When the clothes label reads: permanent press, do not put it in the dryer; hang them up to dry.*
___ Si la etiqueta de la ropa dice: permanent press (planchado permanente) , no ponerla en la secadora, cuélguela para secar al aire.

10. *Don't hang knitted garments, it pulls them out of shape. Fold them and store them in a drawer.*
___ No colgar ropa tejida ya que se ve sin forma, doblarla y guardarla en un cajón.

11. *When you get gum on your clothes, put them in a plastic bag and freeze, then the gum will come off easily.*
___ Si le cae goma de mascar en la ropa, ponerla en una bolsa de plástico y después en el friser, esto lo ayudará a que salga más fácilmente.

12. *If you find it hard to clean the wax off the candlesticks, put them it in the freezer for a while and then pull the wax off.*
___ Si le es difícil limpiar la cera del candelabro póngalo en el friser por un rato y después despégelo.

13. *If you get pen marks on your formica counter, table, etc. wipe it off with alcohol.*
___ Si tiene marcas de tinta en la fórmica de su mostrador, mesa etc. límpielo con un poco de alcohol.

Here is some space for you to add more tips:

Cómo atender el teléfono?
How to answer the telephone
(Jau to answer di telefon)

___ No está:	___ *not home:* *(Not jom.)*
_____ ya viene:	_____ *is coming:* *(Is comin.)*
Aló:	*Hello:* *(Jelou)*
Ambulancia:	*Ambulance:* *(Embiulens.)*
Auxilio/socorro/ayúdeme:	*Help, Help me:* *(Jelp - Jelp mi)*
Bomberos:	*Firemen:* *(Faiermen)*
Comiendo:	*Eating:* *(Itin.)*
Con amigo/a:	*With friend:* *(Wis frend.)*
Cuándo viene a la casa?:	*When are you coming home?:*
	(Wuen ar yu comin jom?)
De compras:	*Shopping:* *(Shapin.)*
De viaje:	*Out of town:* *(Aut of taun.)*
Déje su número:	*Leave your number please:* *(Liv*
	namber plis.)
Déje un mensaje:	*Leave a message please:* *(Liv el*
	mesach plis.)
Deletrée:	*Spell please:* *(Espel plis.)*
Despacio:	*Slow please:* *(Slou plis.)*
Doctor:	*Doctor:* *(Dactor)*
Durmiendo:	*Sleeping:* *(Slipin.)*
El sr. No está:	*Mr. --- not home:* *(Mister not*
	jom.)
Emergencia:	*Emergency:* *(Emerilensi.)*
En el baño:	*In the bathroom:* *(In di basrum.)*
Enfermo:	*Sick:* *(Sik.)*
Estoy perdido:	*I am lost:* *(Ayam lost)*
Familia _____	_____ *residence:*
Residencia _____ :	*(_____ residens.)*
Fuego:	*Fire:* *(Faier.)*

Habla Ud. español?:	Do you speak Spanish?: *(**Do you spik Spanish?)***
Hospital:	Hospital: *(**Jaspitol)***
Importante:	Important: *(**Important.)***
La alarma:	The alarm: *(**Di alarm.)***
La otra línea:	The other line: *(**Di oder lain.)***
La sra. No está:	Mrs. --- not home: *(**Mises not jom.)***
Llame después:	Call later: *(**Col leiter.)***
Llame otra vez:	Call again: *(**Col egen.)***
No entiendo/comprendo:	I don't understand: *(**Ai dont anderstand.)***
No hablo inglés:	I don't speak English: *(**Ai dont spik inglish.)***
Ocupado:	Busy *(**Bisi.)***
Oficina:	Office: *(**Ofis.)***
Operadora:	Operator: *(**Opereitor.)***
Peligro:	Danger: *(**Deinyer)***
Perdón:	I'm sorry: *(**Ayam sorri.)***
Policía:	Police: *(**Polis.)***
Problema:	Problem: *(**Prablem.)***
Qué quiere decir?:	What does that mean?: *(**Wuat das dat min?)***
Quién llama?:	Who's calling?: *(**Jus colin?)***
Repita:	Repeat please: *(**Ripit plis.)***
Trabajo:	Work: *(**Wuork.)***
Un momento:	One moment please: *(**Wan momen plis.)***
Venga para acá:	Come here please: *(**Com jir plis.)***
Yo no sé:	I don't know: *(**Ai dont nou.)***

How to answer the telephone?
(Jau to answer di telefon)
Cómo atender el teléfono

_____ not home: *(Not jom.)*   _____ No está:

_____ is coming: *(Is comin.)*   _____ ya viene:

_____ residence: Familia _____

(_____ *residens.)*   Residencia _____ :

Ambulance: *(Embiulens.)*   Ambulancia:

Busy : *(Bisi.)*   Ocupado:

Call again: *(Col egen.)*   Llame otra vez:

Call later: *(Col leiter.)*   Llame después:

Come here please: *(Com jir plis.)*   Venga para acá:

Danger: *(Deinyer)*   Peligro:

Do you speak Spanish?: *(Do you spik Spanish?)*

    Habla Ud. español?

Doctor: *(Dactor)*   Doctor:

Eating: *(Itin.)*   Comiendo:

Emergency: *(Emerllensi.)*   Emergencia:

Fire: *(Faier.)*   Fuego:

Firemen: *(Faiermen)*   Bomberos:

Hello: *(Jelou)*   Aló:

Help, Help me: *(Jelp - Jelp mi)* Auxilio/socorro/ayúdeme:

Hospital: *(Jaspitol)*   Hospital:

I am lost: *(Ayam lost)*   Estoy perdido:

I don't know: *(Ai dont nou.)*   Yo no sé:

I don't speak English: *(Ai dont spik inglish.)*

    No hablo inglés:

I don't understand: *(Ai dont anderstand.)*

    No entiendo/comprendo:

I'm sorry: *(Ayam sorri.)*   Perdón:

Important: *(Important.)*   Importante:

In the bathroom: *(In di basrum.)*   En el baño:

Leave a message please: **(Liv el mesach plis.)**

Déje un mensaje:

Leave number please: **(Liv namber plis.)**

Déje su número:

Mr. --- not home: **(Mister not jom.)** El sr. No está:

Mrs. --- not home: **(Mises not jom.)** La sra. No está:

Office: **(Ofis.)** Oficina:

One moment please: **(Wan moment plis.)**

Un momento:

Operator: **(Opereitor.)** Operadora:

Out of town: **(Aut of taun.)** De viaje:

Police: **(Polis.)** Policía:

Problem: **(Prablem.)** Problema:

Repeat please: **(Ripit plis.)** Repita:

Shopping: **(Shapin.)** De compras:

Sick: **(Sik.)** Enfermo:

Sleeping: **(Slipin.)** Durmiendo:

Slow please: **(Slou plis.)** Despacio:

Spell please: **(Espel plis.)** Deletrée:

The alarm: **(Di alarm.)** La alarma:

The other line: **(Di oder lain.)** La otra línea:

What does that mean? **(Wuat das dat min?)**

Qué quiere decir?:

When are you coming home? **(Wuen ar yu comin jom?)**

Cuándo viene a la casa?:

Who's calling? **(Jus colin?)** Quién llama?:

With friend: **(Wis frend.)** Con amigo/a:

Work: **(Wuork.)** Trabajo:

Abecedario:
A-B-C

A:	ei
B:	bi
C:	si
D:	di
E:	i
F:	ef
G:	gi
H:	eich
I:	ai
J:	llei
K:	kei
L:	el
M:	em
N:	en
O:	ou
P:	pi
Q:	kiu
R:	ar
S:	es
T:	ti
U:	yu
V:	vi
W:	dabel yu
X:	ex
Y:	wai (guai)
Z:	zi

Números:
Numbers
(nambers)

1:	*One: **(Wan):***	Uno:
2:	*Two: **(Tu):***	Dos:
3:	*Three: **(Tri):***	Tres:
4:	*Four: **(For):***	Cuatro:
5:	*Five: **(Faiv):***	Cinco:
6:	*Six: **(Six):***	Seis:
7.	*Seven: **(Seven):***	Siete:
8:	*Eight: **(Eit):***	Ocho:
9:	*Nine: **(Nain):***	Nueve:
10:	*Ten: **(Ten):***	Diez:
0:	*Zero: **(Sirou - Ó - Ou)***	Cero:

100:	*Hundred: **(Jandred):***	Cien:
1,000:	*Thousand: **(Tausen):***	Mil:
1,000,000:	*Million: **(Milion):***	Millón:

Colores
Colors
(Colors)

Amarillo:	Yellow: *(Yelou)*
Anaranjado:	Orange: *(Oranch)*
Azul:	Blue: *(Blu)*
Beige:	Beige: *(Belg)*
Blanco:	White: *(Wait)*
Café/Marrón/Carmelita:	Brown: *(Braun)*
Claro:	Light: *(Lait)*
Dorado:	Gold: *(Gold)*
Gris:	Gray: *(Grei)*
Melocotón:	Peach: *(Pich)*
Morado:	Purple: *(Perpel)*
Negro:	Black: *(Blak)*
Obscuro:	Dark: *(Dark)*
Plateado:	Silver: *(Silver)*
Rojo:	Red: *(Red)*
Rosado:	Pink: *(Pink)*
Transparente:	Clear : *(Transparent) (Clir)*
Verde:	Green: *(Grin)*

Colors
(Colors)
Colores

Beige: *(Beig)*	Beige:
Black: *(Blak)*	Negro:
Blue: *(Blu)*	Azul:
Brown: *(Braun)*	Café/Marrón/Carmelita:
Clear : *(Transparent) (Clir)*	Transparente:
Dark: *(Dark)*	Obscuro:
Gold: *(Gold)*	Dorado:
Gray: *(Grei)*	Gris:
Green: *(Grin)*	Verde:
Light: *(Lait)*	Claro:
Orange: *(Oranch)*	Anaranjado:
Peach: *(Pich)*	Melocotón:
Pink: *(Pink)*	Rosado:
Purple: *(Perpel)*	Morado:
Red: *(Red)*	Rojo:
Silver: *(Silver)*	Plateado:
White: *(Wait)*	Blanco:
Yellow: *(Yelou)*	Amarillo:

Días de la semana
Days of the week
(Deis of di wik)

Lunes:	Monday: *(Mandei)*
Martes:	Tuesday: *(Tusdei)*
Miércoles:	Wednesday: *(Wensdei)*
Jueves:	Thursday: *(Sursdei)*
Viernes:	Friday: *(Fraidei)*
Sábado:	Saturday: *(Saturdei)*
Domingo:	Sunday: *(Sandei)*
Día:	Day: *(Dei)*
Semana:	Week: *(Wik)*

Partes del día
Parts of the day
(Parts of di dei)

Mañana:	Morning: *(Mornin)*
Tarde:	Afternoon: *(Afternun)*
Noche:	Night: *(Nait)*
Hora:	Hour: *(Aguer)*
Minuto:	Minute: *(Minet)*
Segundo:	Second: *(Second)*
A.M.:	a.m.: *(El-Em)*
P.M.:	p.m. *(Pi-Em)*

Meses
Months
(Mons)

Enero:	January: *(Llanuari)*
Febrero:	February: *(Februari)*
Marzo:	March: *(March)*
Abril:	April: *(Elpril)*
Mayo:	May: *(Mey)*
Junio:	June: *(Yun)*
Julio:	July: *(Yulai)*
Agosto:	August: *(Ogost)*
Septiembre:	September: *(September)*
Octubre:	October: *(October)*
Noviembre:	November: *(November)*
Diciembre:	December: *(Dicember)*
Año:	Year: *(Yir)*
Temperatura:	Temperature: *(Temperchur)*
Lloviendo:	Raining: *(Reinin)*
Viento:	Windy: *(Wuindi)*
Nevando:	Snowing: *(Snouin)*
Nublado:	Cloudy: *(Claudi)*
Frío:	Cold - Cool: *(Cold - Kul)*
Calor:	Hot: *(Jat)*
Húmedo:	Humid: *(Jiumid)*
Seco:	Dry: *(Drai)*

Partes de una casa:
Parts of the house:
(Parts of di jaus)

Alfombra:	Carpet: *(Carpet)*
Ante-comedor:	Breakfast room: *(Brekfast rum)*
Arbol:	Tree: *(Tri)*
Baño:	Bathroom: *(Basrum)*
Bar:	Bar. *(Bar)*
Biblioteca:	Library: *(Laibreri)*
Bombillo/Foco:	Light bulb: *(Lait bolv)*
Cerca:	Fence: *(Fens)*
Chimenea:	Chimney: *(Chimeni)*
Closet:	Closet: *(Closet)*
Cocina:	Kitchen: *(Kichen)*
Comedor:	Dining room: *(Danin rum)*
Correo:	Mailbox: *(Meilbox)*
Cuarto de visitas (Dormitorio):	Guest room: *(Ges rum)*
Cuarto/Dormitorio/Recámara:	Bedroom: *(Bedrum)*
Escalera:	Steps/Stair : *(Esteps/Ester)*
Escalón:	Step: *(Estep)*
Garaje:	Garage: *(Garach)*
Jardín:	Garden: *(Garden)*
Lavadero/Cuarto de lavar:	Laundry room: *(Laundri rum)*
Oficina:	Office: *(Ofis)*
Pared:	Wall: *(Wol)*
Pasillo:	Hall: *(Jol)*
Patio:	Backyard: *(Bakyard)*
Piscina/Alberca:	Pool: *(Pul)*
Piso de cerámica:	Tile floor. *(Tail floor)*
Piso de madera:	Wood floor. *(Wud flor)*
Piso de Plástico:	Linoleum floor. *(Lanolium flor)*
Piso:	Floor. *(Flor)*
Portón:	Porch: *(Porch)*

Puerta:	Door: **(Dor)**
Sala de familia:	Family room: **(Femili rum)**
Sala de juegos:	Play room: **(Plei rum)**
Sala de visitas:	Living room: **(Livin rum)**
Techo:	Roof: **(Ruf)**
Terraza:	Terrace: **(Teras)**
Ventana:	Window: **(Windou)**
Zacate/Yarda/Grama:	Grass: **(Gras)**

Parts of the house
(Parts of di jaus)
Partes de una casa

Backyard: *(Bakyard)*	Patio:
Bar: *(Bar)*	Bar:
Bathroom: *(Basrum)*	Baño:
Bedroom: *(Bedrum)*	Cuarto/Dormitorio/Recámara:
Breakfast room: *(Brekfast rum)*	Ante-comedor:
Carpet: *(Carpet)*	Alfombra:
Chimney: *(Chimeni)*	Chimenea:
Closet: *(Closet)*	Closet:
Dining room: *(Danin rum)*	Comedor:
Door: *(Dor)*	Puerta:
Family room: *(Femili rum)*	Sala de familia:
Fence: *(Fens)*	Cerca:
Floor: *(Flor)*	Piso:
Garage: *(Garach)*	Garaje:
Garden: *(Garden)*	Jardín:
Grass: *(Gras)*	Zacate/Yarda/Grama:
Guest room: *(Ges rum)*	Cuarto de visitas (Dormitorio):
Hall: *(Jol)*	Pasillo:
Kitchen: *(Kichen)*	Cocina:
Laundry room: *(Laundri rum)*	Lavadero/Cuarto de lavar:
Library: *(Laibreri)*	Biblioteca:
Light bulb: *(Lait bolv)*	Bombillo/Foco:
Linoleum floor: *(Lanolium flor)*	Piso de Plástico:
Living room: *(Livin rum)*	Sala de visitas:
Mailbox: *(Meilbox)*	Correo:
Office: *(Ofis)*	Oficina:
Play room: *(Plei rum)*	Sala de juegos:
Pool: *(Pul)*	Piscina/Alberca:
Porch: *(Porch)*	Portón:
Roof: *(Ruf)*	Techo:

Step: *(Estep)*	Escalón:
Steps/Stair : *(Esteps/Ester)*	Escalera:
Terrace: *(Teras)*	Terraza:
Tile floor. *(Tail floor)*	Piso de cerámica:
Tree: *(Tri)*	Arbol:
Wall: *(Wol)*	Pared:
Window: *(Windou)*	Ventana:
Wood floor. *(Wud flor)*	Piso de madera:

Partes del lavadero/Cuarto de lavar
Parts of the laundry room
(Parts of di laundri rum)

Aspiradora:	Vacuum cleaner: *(Vakium cliner)*
Aspiradora de mano:	Dust Buster: *(Dast Baster)*
Canasto para ropa:	Clothes Basket: *(Clous Basket)*
Detergentes:	Detergents: *(Diterllents)*
Escoba:	Broom: *(Brum)*
Esponja:	Sponge: *(Espanch)*
Friser:	Freezer: *(Frizer)*
Jabones:	Soaps: *(Soups)*
Lavamanos:	Sink: *(Sink)*
Máquina de lavar ropa:	Washing machine: *(Washin machin)*
Plancha:	Iron: *(Airon)*
Secadora:	Dryer: *(Draier)*
Secadora de madera:	Wooden rack: *(Wuden rak)*
Tabla de planchar:	Ironing board: *(Aironin bord)*
Tobo/Cubeta:	Bucket: *(Baket)*
Tobo/Cubeta:	Water pail: *(Water peil)*
Trapeador/Mapeador:	Mop: *(Map)*

Parts of the laundry room
(Parts of di laundri rum)
Partes del lavadero/Cuarto de lavar

Broom: *(Brum)* Escoba:

Bucket: *(Baket)* Tobo/Cubeta:

Clothes Basket: *(Clous Basket)* Canasto para ropa:

Detergents: *(Diterllents)* Detergentes:

Dust Buster: *(Dast Baster)* Aspiradora de mano:

Dryer: *(Draler)* Secadora:

Freezer: *(Frizer)* Friser:

Iron: *(Airon)* Plancha:

Ironing board: *(Aironin bord)* Tabla de planchar:

Mop: *(Map)* Trapeador/Mapeador:

Sink: *(Sink)* Lavamanos:

Soaps: *(Soups)* Jabones:

Sponge: *(Espanch)* Esponja:

Vacuum cleaner: *(Vakium cliner)*

  Aspiradora:

Washing machine: *(Washin machin)*

  Máquina de lavar ropa:

Water pail: *(Water pell)* Tobo/Cubeta:

Wooden rack: *(Wuden rak)* Secadora de madera:

Partes de una sala
Parts of the living room
(Parts of di livin rum)

Adorno:	*Ornament*: *(Ornament)*
Candelabro:	*Candelabra*: *(Kendelabra)*
Cenicero:	*Ashtray*: *(Ashtrei)*
Centro de mesa:	*Centerpiece*: *(Senterpis)*
Chimenea:	*Fireplace* :*(Faier pleis)*
Cuadro:	*Picture*: *(Pichur)*
Estatua:	*Statue*: *(Statiu)*
Florero:	*Flower vase*: *(Flauer veis)*
Flor:	*Flower*: *(Flauer)*
Leña:	*Firewood*: *(Faier wud)*
Mesa de juego:	*Game table*: *(Geim teibel)*
Mesa:	*Table/Coffee table*: *(Kofi teibel)*
Pedestal:	*Pedestal/Stand*:
	(Pedestol/Stend)
Piano:	*Piano*: *(Piano)*
Pintura:	*Painting*: *(Peintin)*
Silla:	*Chair*: *(Cher)*
Sofá:	*Couch*: *(Kauch)*
Tapete:	*Area rug*: *(Erea rag)*
Televisión:	*T.V.*: *(Tivi)*
Vidio-casetera:	*V.C.R.*: *(Visiar)*

Parts of the living room
(Parts of di livin rum)
Partes de una sala

Area rug: *(Erea rag)*   Tapete:

Ashtray: *(Ashtrei)*   Cenicero:

Candelabra: *(Kendelabra)*   Candelabro:

Centerpiece: *(Senterpis)*   Centro de mesa:

Chair: *(Cher)*   Silla:

Couch: *(Kauch)*   Sofá:

Fireplace : *(Faier pleis)*   Chimenea:

Firewood: *(Faier wud)*   Leña:

Flower vase: *(Flauer veis)*   Florero:

Flower: *(Flauer)*   Flor:

Game table: *(Geim teibel)*   Mesa de juego:

Ornament: *(Ornament)*   Adorno:

Painting: *(Peintin)*   Pintura:

Pedestal/Stand: *(Pedestol/Stend)*

       Pedestal:

Piano: *(Piano)*   Piano:

Picture: *(Pichur)*   Cuadro:

Statue: *(Statiu)*   Estatua:

Table/Coffee table: *(Kofi teibel)*   Mesa:

T.V.: *(Tivi)*   Televisión:

V.C.R.: *(Visiar)*   Video-casetera:

Partes de un cuarto - dormitorio - recámara
Parts of a bedroom
(Parts of ei bedrum)

Alarma:	Alarm: *(Alarm)*
Alfombra:	Carpet: *(Carpet)*
Almohada:	Pillow: *(Pilou)*
Armario:	Wardrobe: *(Guar-roub)*
Basurero:	Trash can: *(Trash ken)*
Buró/Mesa de noche:	Night stand: *(Nait sten)*
Cama:	Bed: *(Bed)*
Closet:	Closet: *(Closet)*
Colcha/Cobija:	Blanket: *(Blanket)*
Cortina:	Drapes: *(Dreips)*
Cómoda/Repisa:	Chest of drawers: *(Chest of drous)*
Cuaderno:	Notebook: *(Noutbuk)*
Cuadro:	Picture: *(Pichur)*
Cubre-cama:	Bedspread: *(Bedspred)*
Equipo de música:	Stereo: *(Estereo)*
Escritorio:	Desk: *(Desk)*
Espejo:	Mirror: *(Mirror)*
Funda/Sábana para almohada:	Pillow case: *(Pilou keis)*
Gancho de ropa:	Hanger: *(Jenger)*
Juego:	Game: *(Geim)*
Juguete:	Toy: *(Toi)*
Lámpara de noche:	Night light: *(Nait lait)*
Lámpara:	Lamp: *(Lemp)*
Librero:	Book shelf: *(Buk shel)*
Libro:	Book: *(Buk)*
Mesa:	Table: *(Teibel)*
Persiana:	Blinds: *(Blains)*
Planta/Mata:	Plant: *(Plent)*
Radio:	Radio: *(Redio)*

Reloj:	Clock: *(Clak)*
Repizas/Estante:	Shelf: *(Shel)*
Revistero:	Magazine rack: *(Magasin rak)*
Ropa:	Clothes: *(Clous)*
Sábanas:	Sheets: *(Shits)*
Silla:	Chair: *(Cher)*
Teléfono:	Telephone: *(Telefon)*
Televisión:	T.V.: *(Tivi)*
Tocador:	Dresser: *(Dreser)*
Video-casetera:	VCR: *(Visiar)*
Ventilador:	Fan: *(Fen)*
Zapatero:	Shoe rack: *(Shu rak)*

Parts of a bedroom
(Parts of ei bedrum)
Partes de un cuarto - dormitorio - recámara

Alarm: *(Alarm)*	Alarma:
Bed: *(Bed)*	Cama:
Bedspread: *(Bedspred)*	Cubre-cama:
Blanket: *(Blanket)*	Colcha/Cobija:
Blinds: *(Blains)*	Persiana:
Book shelf: *(Buk shel)*	Librero:
Book: *(Buk)*	Libro:
Carpet: *(Carpet)*	Alfombra:
Chair: *(Cher)*	Silla:
Chest of drawers: *(Chest of drous)*	
	Cómoda/Repisa:
Clock: *(Clak)*	Reloj:
Closet: *(Closet)*	Closet:
Clothes: *(Clous)*	Ropa:
Desk: *(Desk)*	Escritorio:
Drapes: *(Dreips)*	Cortina:
Dresser: *(Dreser)*	Tocador:
Fan: *(Fen)*	Ventilador:
Game: *(Geim)*	Juego:
Hanger: *(Jenger)*	Gancho de ropa:
Lamp: *(Lemp)*	Lámpara:
Magazine rack: *(Magasin rak)*	Revistero:
Mirror: *(Mirror)*	Espejo:
Night light: *(Nait lait)*	Lámpara de noche:
Night stand: *(Nait sten)*	Buró/Mesa de noche:
Notebook: *(Noutbuk)*	Cuaderno:
Picture: *(Pichur)*	Cuadro:
Pillow case: *(Pilou keis)*	Funda/Sábana para almohada:
Pillow: *(Pilou)*	Almohada:
Plant: *(Plent)*	Planta/Mata:

Radio: *(Redio)*	Radio:
Sheets: *(Shits)*	Sábanas:
Shelf: *(Shel)*	Repizas/Estante:
Shoe rack: *(Shu rak)*	Zapatero:
Stereo: *(Estereo)*	Equipo de música:
T.V.: *(Tivi)*	Televisión:
Table: *(Teibel)*	Mesa:
Telephone: *(Telefon)*	Teléfono:
Toy: *(Toi)*	Juguete:
Trash can: *(Trash ken)*	Basurero:
VCR : *(Visiar)*	Video-casetera:
Wardrobe: *(Guar-roub)*	Armario:

Ropa
Clothes
(Clous)

Abrigo:	Coat: *(Cout)*
Anillo:	Ring: *(Ring)*
Arete/Sarcillo:	Earring: *(Iring)*
Bata:	Robe: *(Roub)*
Blusa:	Blouse: *(Blaus)*
Bota:	Boot: *(But)*
Botón:	Button: *(Baton)*
Broche:	Pin: *(Pin)*
Bufanda:	Scarf: *(Scarf)*
Cachucha:	Cap: *(Cap)*
Cadena/Collar:	Necklace: *(Neclas)*
Camisa:	Shirt: *(Shert)*
Camiseta/Franela:	T-shirt: *(Ti-shert)*
Cartera/Bolso:	Purse: *(Pers)*
Chaleco:	Vest: *(Vest)*
Chaqueta:	Jacket: *(Llaket)*
Chaqueta de piel:	Fur coat: *(Fer cout)*
Cierre/Cremallera:	Zipper: *(Siper)*
Corbata:	Tie: *(Tai)*
Correa/Cinturón/Cinto:	Belt: *(Belt)*
Dormilona:	Night gown: *(Nait gaun)*
Faja:	Girdle: *(Gerdel)*
Falda:	Skirt: *(Eskert)*
Fondo/Combinación:	Slip: *(Slip)*
Gancho:	Hanger: *(Jenger)*
Guantes:	Gloves: *(Gloubs)*
Hombreras:	Shoulder pads: *(Shoulder pads)*
Impermeable:	Raincoat: *(Rein cout)*
Interiores/Calzoncillos:	Underwear: *(Anderwuer)*

Joyas:	Jewelry: *(Yuleri)*
Lentes/Gafas:	Glasses: *(Glases)*
Medias de nailon:	Panty hose: *(Penti jous)*
Medias:	Socks: *(Saks)*
Pantaletas:	Panties: *(Pentis)*
Pantalón corto:	Shorts: *(Shorts)*
Pantalón de mezclilla:	Jeans: *(Llins)*
Pantalón:	Pants: *(Pents)*
Pantuflas/Sapatillas:	Slippers: *(Slipers)*
Pañuelo:	Handkerchief: *(Jendkerchif)*
Pijamas:	Pajamas: *(Pallamas)*
Pulsera:	Bracelet: *(Breislet)*
Reloj:	Watch: *(Wuach)*
Sandalia:	Sandal: *(Sendol)*
Sombrero:	Hat: *(Jat)*
Sombrilla/Paraguas:	Umbrella: *(Ambrela)*
Sostén/Brasier:	Bra: *(Bra)*
Sueter/Chamarra:	Sweater: *(Sueter)*
Traje de baño:	Bathing suit: *(Beidin sut)*
Traje/Flux:	Suit: *(Sut)*
Velcro:	Velcro: *(Velcro)*
Vestido:	Dress: *(Dres)*
Zapatos:	Shoe: *(Shu)*

Clothes
(Clous)
Ropa

Bathing suit: *(Beidin sut)*	Traje de baño:
Belt: *(Belt)*	Correa/Cinturón/Cinto:
Blouse: *(Blaus)*	Blusa:
Boot: *(But)*	Bota:
Bra: *(Bra)*	Sostén/Brasier:
Bracelet: *(Breislet)*	Pulsera:
Button: *(Baton)*	Botón:
Cap: *(Cap)*	Cachucha:
Coat: *(Cout)*	Abrigo:
Dress: *(Dres)*	Vestido:
Earring: *(Iring)*	Arete/Sarcillo:
Fur coat: *(Fer cout)*	Chaqueta de piel:
Girdle: *(Gerdel)*	Faja:
Glasses: *(Glases)*	Lentes/Gafas:
Gloves: *(Gloubs)*	Guantes:
Handkerchief: *(Jendkerchif)*	Pañuelo:
Hanger: *(Jenger)*	Gancho:
Hat: *(Jat)*	Sombrero:
Jacket: *(Llaket)*	Chaqueta:
Jeans: *(Llins)*	Pantalón de mezclilla:
Jewelry: *(yuleri)*	Joyas:
Necklace: *(Neclas)*	Cadena/Collar:
Night gown: *(Nalt gaun)*	Dormilona:
Pajamas: *(Pallamas)*	Pijamas:
Panties: *(Pentis)*	Pantaletas:
Pants: *(Pents)*	Pantalón:
Panty hose: *(Penti jous)*	Medias de nailon:
Pin: *(Pin)*	Broche:
Purse: *(Pers)*	Cartera/Bolso:
Raincoat: *(Rein cout)*	Impermeable:

Ring: *(Ring)*	Anillo:
Robe: *(Roub)*	Bata:
Sandal: *(Sendol)*	Sandalia:
Scarf: *(Scarf)*	Bufanda:
Shirt: *(Shert)*	Camisa:
Shoe: *(Shu)*	Zapatos:
Shorts: *(Shorts)*	Pantalón corto:
Shoulder pads: *(Shoulder pads)*	
	Hombreras:
Skirt: *(Eskert)*	Falda:
Slip: *(Slip)*	Fondo/Combinación:
Slippers: *(Slipers)*	Pantuflas/Sapatillas:
Socks: *(Saks)*	Medias:
Suit: *(Sut)*	Traje/Flux:
Sweater: *(Sueter)*	Sueter/Chamarra:
T-shirt: *(Ti-shert)*	Camiseta/Franela:
Tie: *(Tai)*	Corbata:
Umbrella: *(Ambrela)*	Sombrilla/Paraguas:
Underwear: *(Anderwuer)*	Interiores/Calzoncillos:
Velcro: *(Velcro)*	Velcro:
Vest: *(Vest)*	Chaleco:
Watch: *(Wuach)*	Reloj:
Zipper: *(Siper)*	Cierre/Cremallera:

Partes del baño
Parts of the bathroom
(Parts of di basrum)

Afeitadora:	*Shaver.* *(Shelver)*
Agarradero de papel t./Papelero:	*Toilet paper holder.* *(Tualet peiper holder)*
Algodón:	*Cotton ball:* *(Katon bol)*
Basurero:	*Trash can:* *(Trash kan)*
Bide:	*Bidet:* *(Bide)*
Botica/Gabinete de medicina:	*Medicine chest:* *(Medisin chest)*
Cepillo de dientes:	*Tooth brush:* *(Tus brash)*
Cepillo de pelo:	*Hair brush:* *(Jer brash)*
Cortina de baño:	*Shower curtain:· (Shawuer cortan)*
Crema:	*Cream:* *(Crim)*
Espejo:	*Mirror.* *(Miror)*
Excusado/Poseta/ Inodoro:	*Toilet:* *(Toilet)*
Flor:	*Flower.* *(Flauer)*
Grifo/Chorro:	*Faucet:* *(Foset)*
Hojilla:	*Razor.* *(Reisor)*
Jabón:	*Soap:* *(Soup)*
Jabonera:	*Soap dish:* *(Soup dish)*
Klinex/papel sutil:	*Kleenex/Tissue paper.* *(Tishu peiper)*
Lavamano:	*Sink:* *(Sink)*
Luces:	*Lights:* *(Laits)*
Luz:	*Light:* *(Lait)*
Maquillaje:	*Make-up:* *(Meikap)*
Papel tualet/sanitario:	*Toilet paper.* *(Tualet peiper)*
Pasta de dientes:	*Tooth paste:* *(Tus peist)*
Peine:	*Comb:* *(Com)*
Perfume/Colonia:	*Perfume/Cologne:* *(Perfium/Colon)*

Pesa:	Scale: *(Skeil)*
Pintura de uñas:	Nail polish: *(Neil polish)*
Pinzas:	Tweezers: *(Tuisers)*
Plantas:	Plants: *(Plents)*
Polvo/Talco:	Powder: *(Pauder)*
Regadera/Ducha:	Shower: *(Shawuer)*
Ropero/Canasto de ropa sucia:	Hamper: *(Jemper)*
Secadora de pelo:	Hair dryer: *(Jer drayer)*
Shampú:	Shampoo: *(Shampu)*
Silla:	Chair: *(Cher)*
Tapete:	Bath mat: *(Bas mat)*
Tijeras:	Scissors: *(Sisors)*
Tina/Bañera:	Bath tub: *(Bas tab)*
Toalla:	Towel: *(Tawuel)*
Toallera:	Towel rack: *(Tawuel rak)*
Tocador/Peinadora:	Vanity: *(Vaniti)*
Vaso:	Cup: *(Cap)*
Vestuario:	Dressing room: *(Dresin rum)*

Parts of the bathroom
(Parts of di basrum)
Partes del baño

Bath mat: *(Bas mat)*	Tapete:
Bath tub: *(Bas tab)*	Tina/Bañera:
Bidet: *(Bide)*	Bide:
Chair: *(Cher)*	Silla:
Comb: *(Com)*	Peine:
Cotton ball: *(Katon bol)*	Algodón:
Cream: *(Crim)*	Crema:
Cup: *(Cap)*	Vaso:
Dressing room: *(Dresin rum)*	Vestuario:
Faucet: *(Foset)*	Grifo/Chorro:
Flower: *(Flauer)*	Flor:
Hair brush: *(Jer brash)*	Cepillo de pelo:
Hair dryer: *(Jer drayer)*	Secadora de pelo:
Hamper: *(Jemper)*	Ropero/Canasto de ropa sucia:
Kleenex/Tissue paper: *(Tishu peiper)*	
	Klinex/papel sutil:
Light: *(Lait)*	Luz:
Lights: *(Laits)*	Luces:
Make-up: *(Meikap)*	Maquillaje:
Medicine chest: *(Medisin chest)*	
	Botica/Gabinete de medicina:
Mirror: *(Miror)*	Espejo:
Nail polish: *(Neil polish)*	Pintura de uñas:
Perfume/Cologne: *(Perfium/Colon)*	
	Perfume/Colonia:
Plants: *(Plents)*	Plantas:
Powder: *(Pauder)*	Polvo/Talco:
Razor: *(Reisor)*	Hojilla:
Scale: *(Skeil)*	Pesa:
Scissors: *(Sisors)*	Tijeras:

Shampoo: *(Shampu)*	Shampú:
Shaver: *(Sheiver)*	Afeitadora:
Shower curtain: *(Shawuer cortan)*	
	Cortina de baño:
Shower: *(Shawuer)*	Regadera/Ducha:
Sink: *(Sink)*	Lavamano:
Soap dish: *(Soup dish)*	Jabonera:
Soap: *(Soup)*	Jabón:
Toilet paper holder: *(Tualet peiper holder)*	
	Agarradero de papel t./Papelero:
Toilet paper: *(Tualet peiper)*	Papel tualet/sanitario:
Toilet: *(Toilet)*	Excusado/Poseta/ Inodoro:
Tooth brush: *(Tus brash)*	Cepillo de dientes:
Tooth paste: *(Tus peist)*	Pasta de dientes:
Towel rack: *(Tawuel rak)*	Toallera:
Towel: *(Tawuel)*	Toalla:
Trash can: *(Trash kan)*	Basurero:
Tweezers: *(Tuisers)*	Pinzas:
Vanity: *(Vaniti)*	Tocador/Peinadora:

Cosas de la cocina:
Things in the kitchen:
(Zings in di kitchen):

Ablandador de carne:	Meat tenderizer *(Mit tenderaiser)*
Abre latas:	Can opener. *(Ken opener)*
Azucarera:	Sugar bowl: *(Shugar boul)*
Bandeja/charola (Para cocinar):	Cooking sheet: *(Cukin shit)*
Bandeja/charola (Para servir):	Tray: *(Trei)*
Bar:	Bar. *(Bar)*
Basurero:	Garbage can/trash: *(Trash/garbich)*
Batidora:	Mixer. *(Mixer)*
Botella:	Bottle: *(Batel)*
Cafetera:	Coffee maker. *(Kofi meiker)*
Canasta:	Basket: *(Basket)*
Caramelera:	Candy dish: *(Kendi dish)*
Caserola de servir:	Casserole dish: *(Caserol dish)*
Chorro/grifo:	Faucet: *(Foset)*
Closet de comidas:	Pantry: *(Pentri)*
Colador:	Strainer. *(Estreiner)*
Comal/Búdare:	Griddle: *(Gridel)*
Comprimidor de basura:	Trash compacter: *(Trash compactor)*
Congelador/friser:	Freezer: *(Friser)*
Copas (de vino):	Wine cup: *(Wain cap)*
Cremera:	Coffee creamer. *(Cofi creimer)*
Cuchara de servir:	Serving spoon: *(Servin spun)*
Cucharada:	Spoon (Tablespoon): *(Teibelspun)*
Cucharas para medir:	Measuring spoons: *(Meshurin espuns)*
Cuchillo de cortar:	Cutting knife: *(Catin naif)*

Cuchillo eléctrico:	Electric knife: *(Electric naif)*
Cuchillo:	Knife: *(Naif)*
Cuchradita:	Spoon (Teaspoon): *(Tispun)*
Desechador:	Disposal: *(Disposol)*
Embudo:	Funnel: *(Fanel)*
Ensaladera:	Salad bowl: *(Salad boul)*
Envase de plástico:	Tupperware: *(Taperwuer)* *(Plastic container)*
Espátula:	Spatula: *(Spatula)*
Estufa:	Stove: *(Estov)*
Extensión de mesa:	Table leaves: *(Teibel livs)*
Filtro de café:	Coffee filter: *(Kofi filter)*
Frasco/bote:	Jar. *(Llar)*
Frutero:	Fruit dish/bowl: *(Frut dish/bowl)*
Gabinetes:	Cabinet: *(Cabinet)*
Gavetas:	Drawers: *(Drous)*
Heladera:	Ice cream scooper. *(Ais crim scuper)*
Hielera:	Ice bucket: *(Ais baket)*
Hielera:	Ice maker. *(Ais meiker)*
Hornillas:	Burner. *(Berner)*
Horno:	Oven: *(Aven)*
Jarra:	Pitcher. *(Pitcher)*
Lata:	Tin: *(Tin)*
Lava manos:	Sink: *(Sink)*
Lavadora de platos:	Dishwasher. *(Dishwasher)*
Libro de cocina:	Cook book: *(Kuc buk)*
Licuadora:	Blender: *(Blender)*
Mantel:	Tablecloth: *(Teibelclos)*
Manteles individuales:	Placemats: *(Pleismets)*
Mantequillera:	Butter server: *(Bater server)*
Máquina para hacer palomitas:	Corn popper. *(Corn paper)*
Mesa:	Table: *(Teibel)*
Micro-ondas:	Microwave oven: *(Maicroweiv)*
Molde de gelatina:	Gelatin mold: *(Llelatin mold)*

Molde de hornear:	Baking dish: *(Belkin dish)*
Molde para pastel/torta:	Cake pan: *(Keik pen)*
Moldes de galletas:	Cookie cutters: *(Kuki katers)*
Molino:	Grinder: *(Grainder)*
Mostrador:	Counter: *(Caunter)*
Nevera/Refrigerador:	Refrigerator: *(Refrillreitor)*
Olla de baño maría:	Double boiler: *(Dobel boiler)*
Olla de vapor:	Steamer: *(Stimer)*
Olla:	Pot: *(Pat)*
Palillo de dientes:	Tooth pick: *(Tus pik)*
Paño de cocina:	Kitchen towel: *(Kitchen tawuel)*
Parrilla:	Grill: *(Gril)*
Pelador:	Peeler: *(Piler)*
Pimentero:	Pepper shaker: *(Peper sheiker)*
Plancha para waffles:	Waffle iron: *(Wuafel airon)*
Plato:	Plate: *(Pleit)*
Plato de servir:	Serving dish: *(Servin dish)*
Plato hondo:	Soup/cereal bowl: *(Sup/ sirial boul)*
Prensa de ajo:	Garlic press: *(Garlic pres)*
Procesador de comida:	Food processor: *(Fud prosesor)*
Protector de mesa:	Table pad: *(Teibel pad)*
Reloj de cocina:	Timer: *(Taimer)*
Rodillo:	Rolling Pin: *(Rolin pin)*
Salero:	Salt shaker: *(Solt sheiker)*
Sartén:	Skillet: *(Eskilet)*
Salsera:	Gravy Boat: *(Greivi Bout)*
Servilletas:	Napkins: *(Napkins)*
Silla:	Chair: *(Cher)*
Sopera/cucharón:	Ladel: *(Leidel)*
Tabla para cortar:	Cutting board: *(Catin bor)*
Taburete/Banquillo:	Stool: *(Stul)*
Taza de medir:	Measuring cup: *(Meshurin cap)*
Taza:	Cup: *(Cap)*
Tazón:	Bowl: *(Boul)*

Tenazas:	*Tongs:* **(Tongs)**
Tenedor de servir:	*Serving fork:* **(Servin fork)**
Tenedor:	*Fork:* **(Fork)**
Termo:	*Thermos:* **(Sermos)**
Tetera:	*Tea kettle:* **(Ti ketel)**
Toallas de papel:	*Paper towel:* **(Peiper tawuel)**
Tostadora:	*Toaster:* **(Touster)**
Vajilla de diario:	Everyday dishes: **(Evridei dishes)**
Vajilla de lujo:	*China:* **(Chaina)**
Vaso:	*Glass:* **(Glas)**

Things in the kitchen:
(Zings in di kitchen):
Cosas de la cocina:

Baking dish: *(Beikin dish)*	Molde de hornear:
Bar: *(Bar)*	Bar:
Basket: *(Basket)*	Canasta:
Blender: *(Blender)*	Licuadora:
Bottle: *(Batel)*	Botella:
Bowl: *(Boul)*	Tazón:
Burner: *(Berner)*	Hornillas:
Butter server: *(Bater server)*	Mantequillera:
Cabinet: *(Cabinet)*	Gabinetes:
Cake pan: *(Keik pen)*	Molde para pastel/torta:
Can opener: *(Ken opener)*	Abre latas:
Candy dish: *(Kendi dish)*	Caramelera:
Casserole dish: *(Caserol dish)*	Caserola de servir:
China: *(Chaina)*	Vajilla de lujo:
Chair: *(Cher)*	Silla:
Coffee creamer: *(Kofi crimer)*	Cremera:
Coffee filter: *(Kofi filter)*	Filtro de café:
Coffee maker: *(Kofi meiker)*	Cafetera:
Cook book: *(Kuc buk)*	Libro de cocina:
Cookie cutters: *(Kuki katers)*	Moldes de galletas:
Cooking sheet: *(Cukin shit)*	Bandeja/charola (Para cocinar) :
Corn popper: *(Corn paper)*	Máquina para hacer palomitas:
Counter: *(Caunter)*	Mostrador:
Cup: *(Cap)*	Taza:
Cutting board: *(Catin bor)*	Tabla para cortar:
Cutting knife: *(Catin naif)*	Cuchillo de cortar:
Dishwasher: *(Dishwasher)*	Lavadora de platos:
Disposal: *(Disposol)*	Desechador:
Double boiler: *(Dobel boiler)*	Olla de baño maría:
Drawers: *(Drous)*	Gavetas:

Electric knife: *(Electric naif)*   Cuchillo eléctrico:
Everyday dishes: *(Evridei dishes)*

Vajilla de diario:
Faucet: *(Foset)*   Chorro/grifo:
Food processor: *(Fud prosesor)*   Procesador de comida:
Fork: *(Fork)*   Tenedor:
Freezer: *(Friser)*   Congelador/friser:
Fruit dish/bowl: *(Frut dish/bowl)*   Frutero:
Funnel: *(Fanel)*   Embudo:
Garbage can/trash: *(Trash/garbich)*

Basurero:
Garlic press: *(Garlic pres)*   Prensa de ajo:
Gelatin mold: *(Llelatin mold)*   Molde de gelatina:
Glass: *(Glas)*   Vaso:
Gravy boat: *(Greivi bout)*   Salsera:
Griddle: *(Gridel)*   Comal/Budare:
Grill: *(Gril)*   Parrilla:
Grinder: *(Grainder)*   Molino:
Ice bucket: *(Ais bucket)*   Hielera:
Ice cream scooper: *(Ais crim scuper)*

Heladera:
Ice maker: *(Ais meiker)*   Hielera:
Jar: *(Llar)*   Frasco/bote:
Kitchen towel: *(Kitchen tawuel)*   Paño de cocina:
Knife: *(Naif)*   Cuchillo:
Ladel: *(Leidel)*   Sopera/cucharón:
Measuring cup: *(Meshurin cap)* Taza de medir:
Measuring spoons: *(Meshurin espuns)*

Cucharas para medir:
Meat tenderizer:*(Mit tenderaiser)*

Ablandador de carne:
Microwave oven: *(Maicroweiv)*   Micro-ondas:
Mixer: *(Mixer)*   Batidora:
Napkins: *(Napkins)*   Servilletas:
Oven: *(Aven)*   Horno:

Pantry: *(Pentri)*	Closet de comidas:
Paper towel: *(Peiper tawuel)*	Toallas de papel:
Peeler: *(Piler)*	Pelador:
Pepper shaker: *(Peper sheiker)*	Pimentero:
Pitcher: *(Pitcher)*	Jarra:
Placemats: *(Pleismets)*	Manteles individuales:
Plate: *(Pleit)*	Plato:
Pot: *(Pat)*	Olla:
Refrigerator: *(Refrillreitor)*	Nevera/refrigerador:
Rolling Pin: *(Rolin pin)*	Rodillo:
Salad bowl: *(Salad boul)*	Ensaladera:
Salt shaker: *(Solt sheiker)*	Salero:
Serving dish: *(Servin dish)*	Plato de servir:
Serving fork: *(Servin fork)*	Tenedor de servir:
Serving spoon: *(Servin spun)*	Cuchara de servir:
Sink: *(Sink)*	Lava manos:
Skillet: *(Eskilet)*	Sartén:
Soup/cereal bowl: *(Sup/sirial boul)*	
	Plato hondo:
Spatula: *(Spatula)*	Espátula:
Spoon (Tablespoon): *(Teibelspun)*	
	Cucharada:
Spoon (Teaspoon): *(Tispun)*	Cuchradita:
Steamer: *(Stimer)*	Olla de vapor:
Stool: *(Stul)*	Taburete/Banquillo:
Stove: *(Estov)*	Estufa:
Strainer: *(Estreiner)*	Colador:
Sugar bowl: *(Shugar boul)*	Azucarera:
Table leaves: *(Teibel livs)*	Extensión de mesa:
Table pad: *(Teibel pad)*	Protector de mesa:
Table: *(Teibel)*	Mesa:
Tablecloth: *(Teibelclos)*	Mantel:
Tea kettle: *(Ti ketel)*	Tetera:
Thermos: *(Sermos)*	Termo:
Timer: *(Taimer)*	Reloj de cocina:

Tin: *(Tin)*	Lata: .
Toaster: *(Touster)*	Tostadora:
Tongs: *(Tongs)*	Tenazas:
Tooth pick: *(Tus pik)*	Palillo de dientes:
Trash compacter: *(Trash compactor)*	
	Comprimidor de basura:
Tray: *(Trei)*	Bandeja/charola (Para servir) :
Tupperware (Plastic container): *(Taperwuer)*	
	Envase de plástico:
Waffle iron: *(Wuafel airon)*	Plancha para waffles:
Wine cup: *(Wain cap)*	Copas (de vino)

Comidas, especies etc.
Foods, spices etc.
(Fuds, spaises etc.)

Frutas:	Fruit: (Frut)
Cereza:	Cherry: (Cherri)
Ciruela pasa:	Prunes: (Pruns)
Ciruela:	Plum: (Plam)
Coco:	Coconut: (Coconat)
Durazno:	Apricot: (Eipricot)
Ensalada de fruta:	Fruit salad: (Frut salad)
Fresa:	Strawberry: (Estroberi)
Limón:	Lemon/lime: (Lemon - laim)
Manzana:	Apple: (Apel)
Melocotón:	Peach: (Pich)
Melón:	Cantaloupe: (Kenteloup)
Mora:.	Blackberry: (Blakberri)
Naranja:	Orange: (Oranch)
Pasita:	Raisin: (Reisin)
Pera:	Pear: (Per)
Piña:	Pineapple: (Painapel)
Plátano/banana/guineo:	Banana: (Banana)
Toronja:	Grapefruit: (Greipfrut)
Uva:	Grape: (Greip)

Verdura/vegetales:	Vegetable: (Vechtebol)
Alcachofas:	Artichokes: (Artichoks)
Berenjena:	Eggplant: (Egplant)
Berro:	Watercress: (Wuatercrest)
Betabel/remolacha:	Beets: (Bits)
Brocoli:	Broccoli: (Brokoli)
Calabacita verde:	Zucchini: (Sukini)
Calabaza:	Pumpkin/Squash: (Pampkin - eskuash)
Camote/Batata:	Sweet potato: (Suit poteito)

Cebolla:	*Onion: **(Anion)***
Cebollín:	*Green onion: **(Grin anion)***
Chicharos/alberjas:	*Peas: **(Pis)***
Coliflor:	*Cauliflower: **(Koliflauer)***
Elote/maíz:	*Corn: **(Corn)***
Espárragos:	*Asparagus: **(Esperrages)***
Espinaca:	*Spinach: **(Espinach)***
Frijoles:	*Beans: **(Bins)***
Hongo:	*Mushroom: **(Mashrum)***
Lechuga:	*Lettuce: **(Letus)***
Nabo:	*Turnip: **(Ternap)***
Papa:	*Potato: **(Poteito)***
Pepino:	*Cucumber: **(Kiukamber)***
Rábano:	*Radish: **(Radish)***
Repollo/col:	*Cabbage: **(Kabech)***
Tomate:	*Tomato: **(Tomeito)***
Vainitas/ejotes:	*Green beans: **(Grin bin)***
Zanahoria:	*Carrot: **(Kerrot)***

Bebidas: *Drinks: **(Drinks)***

Agua:	*Water: **(Wuater)***
Bebida Alcoholica:	*Alcoholic drink: **(Alcojolic drink)***
Café:	*Coffee: **(Cofi)***
Cerveza:	*Beer: **(Bir)***
Chocolateada:	*Chocolate milk: **(Chocolat milk)***
Gaseosa/refresco:	*Soft drink: **(Soft drink)***
Jugo:	*Juice: **(Yus)***
Leche descremada:	*Skim milk: **(Eskim milk)***
Leche evaporada:	*Evaporated milk: **(Evaporetet milk)***
Leche:	*Milk: **(Milk)***
ʼMerengada/batido:	*Shake: **(Sheik)***
Sopa:	*Soup: **(Sup)***
Té:	*Tea: **(Ti)***
Vino:	*Wine: **(Wuain)***

Pan:	Bread: *(Bred)*
Cereal:	Cereal: *(Siriol)*
Galleta:	Cookie: *(Kuki)*
Harina:	Flour: *(Flauer)*
Pan tostado:	Toast: *(Toust)*
Panecillos:	Rolls: *(Rouls)*
Panqueca:	Pancake: *(Pankeik)*
Pastel/torta:	Cake: *(Keik)*

Comida:	Food: *(Fud)*
Aceite:	Oil: *(Oil)*
Arroz:	Rice: *(Rais)*
Atún:	Tuna: *(Tuna)*
Barbacoa:	Barbecue: *(Barbikiu)*
Bistec:	Steak: *(Steik)*
Carne:	Beef: *(Bif)*
Cerdo/cochino:	Pork: *(Pork)*
Chocolate:	Chocolate: *(Chocolat)*
Chuleta:	Chop: *(Chap)*
Consomé:	Broth: *(Bros)*
Crema agria:	Sour Cream: *(Sauer crim)*
Crema:	Cream: *(Krim)*
Crema de maní:	Peanut butter: *(Pinat bater)*
Encurtido:	Pickle: *(Pikel)*
Ensalada:	Salad: *(Salad)*
Espagueti:	Spaghetti: *(Espagueti)*
Fideos:	Noodles: *(Nudels)*
Fruta seca:	Dry fruit: *(Drai frut)*
Gelatina:	Jello/gelatin: *(Llelo - llelatin)*
Helado:	Ice cream: *(Ais krim)*
Huevo:	Egg: *(Eg)*
Jamón:	Ham: *(Jam)*
Leche Condensada:	Condensed milk: *(Condensed milk)*
Macarrones:	Macaroni: *(Makaroni)*

Manteca:	Lard: *(Lard)*
Mantequilla:	Butter: *(Bater)*
Margarina:	Margarine: *(Marllarin)*
Mariscos:	Seafood: *(Sifud)*
Merienda:	Snack: *(Esnak)*
Mermelada:	Jelly: *(LLeli)*
Mostaza:	Mustard: *(Mastard)*
Nueces:	Nuts: *(Nats)*
Pavo:	Turkey: *(Terki)*
Pescado:	Fish: *(Fish)*
Pollo:	Chicken: *(Chiken)*
Pudín:	Pudding: *(Pudin)*
Queso crema:	Cream cheese: *(Crim chis)*
Queso:	Cheese: *(Chis)*
Salsa para ensalada:	Salad Dressing: *(Salad Dresin)*
Salsa:	Gravy: *(Greivi)*
Salsa:	Sauce: *(Sous)*
Tocineta:	Bacon: *(Beicon)*

Especies:	*Spices: **(Espaises)***
Ajo:	Garlic: *(Garlic)*
Azúcar:	Sugar: *(Shugar)*
Bicarbonato de soda:	Baking soda: *(Beikin souda)*
Canela:	Cinnamon: *(Sinamon)*
Catsup:	Catsup: *(Ketchap)*
Cebolla rallada:	Onion flakes: *(Anion fleiks)*
Clavos de comer:	Cloves: *(Cloubs)*
Comino:	Cumin: *(Kiumin)*
Enelo:	Dill: *(Dil)*
Hoja de laurel:	Bay leaf: *(Bei lif)*
Licorera:	Decanter: *(Dicanter)*
Mayonesa:	Mayonnaise: *(Mellones)*
Mostaza:	Mustard: *(Mastard)*
Nuez mozcada:	Nutmeg: *(Natmeg)*
Orégano:	Oregano: *(Oregano)*

Perejil:	Parsley: *(Parsli)*
Pimentón rojo:	Paprika: *(Paprika)*
Pimienta:	Pepper: *(Peper)*
Polvo de hornear:	Baking powder: *(Beikin pauder)*
Sal:	Salt: *(Solt)*
Salsa inglesa:	Worcestershire sauce:
	(Wuorstesher sos)
Salsa japonesa:	Teriyaki sauce: *(Terillaki sos)*
Soya:	Soy sauce: *(Soi sas)*
Vainilla:	Vanilla: *(Vanela)*
Vinagre:	Vinegar: *(Vinager)*
Vino de cocinar:	Cooking wine: *(Kukin wuain)*

Foods, spices etc.
(Fuds, spaises etc.)
Comidas, especies etc.

Fruit: *(Frut)*	Frutas:
Apple: *(Apel)*	Manzana:
Apricot: *(Eipricot)*	Durazno:
Banana: *(Banana)*	Plátano/banana/guineo:
Blackberry: *(Blakberri)*	Mora:
Cantaloupe: *(Kenteloup)*	Melón:
Cherry: *(Cherri)*	Cereza:
Coconut: *(Coconat)*	Coco:
Fruit salad: *(Frut salad)*	Ensalada de fruta:
Grape: *(Greip)*	Uva:
Grapefruit: *(Greipfrut)*	Toronja:
Lemon/lime: *(Lemon - laim)*	Limón:
Orange: *(Oranch)*	Naranja:
Peach: *(Pich)*	Melocotón:
Pear: *(Per)*	Pera:
Pineapple: *(Painapel)*	Piña:
Plum: *(Plam)*	Ciruela:
Prunes: *(Pruns)*	Ciruela pasa:
Raisin: *(Reisin)*	Pasita:
Strawberry: *(Estroberi)*	Fresa:

Vegetable: *(Vechtebol)*	Verdura/vegetales:
Artichokes: *(Artichoks)*	Alcachofas:
Asparagus: *(Esperrages)*	Espárragos:
Beans: *(Bins)*	Frijoles:
Beets: *(Bits)*	Betabel/remolacha:
Broccoli: *(Brokoli)*	Brocoli:
Cabbage: *(Kabech)*	Repollo/col:
Carrot: *(Kerrot)*	Zanahoria:
Cauliflower: *(Koliflauer)*	Coliflor:
Corn: *(Corn)*	Elote/maíz:

Cucumber: *(Kiukamber)*	Pepino:
Eggplant: *(Egplant)*	Berenjena:
Green beans: *(Grin bin)*	Vainitas/ejotes:
Green onion: *(Grin anion)*	Cebollín:
Lettuce: *(Letus)*	Lechuga:
Mushroom: *(Mashrum)*	Hongo:
Onion: *(Anion)*	Cebolla:
Peas: *(Pis)*	Chicharos/alberjas:
Potato: *(Poteito)*	Papa:
Pumpkin/Squash: *(Pampkin - eskuash)*	
	Calabaza:
Radish: *(Radish)*	Rábano:
Spinach: *(Espinach)*	Espinaca:
Sweet potato: *(Suit poteito)*	Camote/Batata:
Tomato: *(Tomeito)*	Tomate:
Turnip: *(Ternap)*	Nabo:
Watercress: *(Wuatercrest)*	Berro:
Zucchini: *(Sukini)*	Calabacita verde:

Drinks: *(Drinks)* Bebidas:

Alcoholic drink: *(Alcojolic drink)*	Bebida Alcóholica:
Beer: *(Bir)*	Cerveza:
Chocolate milk: *(Chocolat milk)*	Chocolateada:
Coffee: *(Cofi)*	Café:
Evaporated milk: *(Evaporetet milk)*	
	Leche evaporada:
Juice: *(Yus)*	Jugo:
Milk: *(Milk)*	Leche:
Shake: *(Sheik)*	Merengada/batido:
Skim milk: *(Eskim milk)*	Leche descremada:
Soft drink: *(Soft drink)*	Gaseosa/refresco:
Soup: *(Sup)*	Sopa:
Tea: *(Ti)*	Té:
Water: *(Wuater)*	Agua:
Wine: *(Wuain)*	Vino:

Bread: **(Bred)**	Pan:
Cake: **(Keik)**	Pastel/torta:
Cereal: **(Siriol)**	Cereal:
Cookie: **(Kuki)**	Galleta:
Flour: **(Flauer)**	Harina:
Pancake: **(Pankeik)**	Panqueca:
Rolls: **(Rouls)**	Panecillos:
Toast: **(Toust)**	Pan tostado:
Food: **(Fud)**	Comida:
Bacon: **(Beicon)**	Tocineta:
Barbecue: **(Barbikiu)**	Barbacoa:
Beef: **(Bif)**	Carne:
Broth: **(Bros)**	Consomé:
Butter: **(Bater)**	Mantequilla:
Cheese: **(Chis)**	Queso:
Chicken: **(Chiken)**	Pollo:
Chocolate: **(Chocolat)**	Chocolate:
Chop: **(Chap)**	Chuleta:
Condensed milk: **(Condensed milk)**	
	Leche condensada:
Cream cheese: **(Crim chis)**	Queso crema:
Cream: **(Krim)**	Crema:
Dry fruit: **(Drai frut)**	Fruta seca:
Egg: **(Eg)**	Hüevo:
Fish: **(Fish)**	Pescado:
Gravy: **(Greivi)**	Salsa:
Ham: **(Jam)**	Jamón:
Ice cream: **(Ais krim)**	Helado:
Jello/gelatin: **(Llelo - llelatin)**	Gelatina:
Jelly: **(LLeli)**	Mermelada:
Lard: **(Lard)**	Manteca:
Macaroni: **(Makaroni)**	Macarrones:
Margarine: **(Marllarin)**	Margarina:
Mustard: **(Mastard)**	Mostaza:

Noodles: *(Nudels)*	Fideos:
Nuts: *(Nats)*	Nueces:
Oil: *(Oil)*	Aceite:
Peanut butter: *(Pinat bater)*	Crema de maní:
Pickle: *(Pikel)*	Encurtido:
Pork: *(Pork)*	Cerdo/cochino:
Pudding: *(Pudin)*	Pudín:
Rice: *(Rais)*	Arroz:
Salad Dressing: *(Salad Dresin)*	Salsa para ensalada:
Salad: *(Salad)*	Ensalada:
Sauce: *(Sous)*	Salsa:
Seafood: *(Sifud)*	Mariscos:
Snack: *(Esnak)*	Merienda:
Sour cream: *(Sauer crim)*	Crema agria:
Spaghetti: *(Espagueti)*	Espagueti:
Steak: *(Steik)*	Bistec:
Tuna: *(Tuna)*	Atún:
Turkey: *(Terki)*	Pavo:

Spices: *(Espaises)*   Especies:

Baking powder: *(Beikin pauder)*	Polvo de hornear:
Baking soda: *(Beikin souda)*	Bicarbonato de soda:
Bay leaf: *(Bei lif)*	Hoja de laurel:
Catsup: *(Ketchap)*	Catsup:
Cinnamon: *(Sinamon)*	Canela:
Cloves: *(Cloubs)*	Clavos de comer:
Cooking wine: *(Kukin wuain)*	Vino de cocinar:
Cumin: *(Kiumin)*	Comino:
Decanter: *(Dicanter)*	Licorera:
Dill: *(Dil)*	Enelo:
Garlic: *(Garlic)*	Ajo:
Mayonnaise: *(Mellones)*	Mayonesa:
Mustard: *(Mastard)*	Mostaza:
Nutmeg: *(Natmeg)*	Nuez mozcada:
Onion flakes: *(Anion fleiks)*	Cebolla rallada:

Oregano: *(Oregano)*	Orégano:
Paprika: *(Paprika)*	Pimentón rojo:
Parsley: *(Parsli)*	Perejil:
Pepper: *(Peper)*	Pimienta:
Salt: *(Solt)*	Sal:
Soy sauce: *(Soi sas)*	Soya:
Sugar: *(Shugar)*	Azúcar:
Teriyaki sauce: *(Terillaki sos)*	Salsa japonesa:
Vanilla: *(Vanela)*	Vainilla:
Vinegar: *(Vinager)*	Vinagre:
Worcestershire sauce: *(Wuorstesher sos)*	
	Salsa inglesa:

Artefactos eléctricos suiches
Switches for electric appliances
(Suitches for electric aplaienses)

Adelantar:	Forward: *(Fowuar)*
Alto:	High: *(Jai)*
Apagar:	Off: *(Of)*
Automático:	Auto: *(Oto)*
	Automatic: *(Automatic)*
Bajo:	Low: *(Lou)*
Borrar:	Erase: *(Ireis)*
Botón:	Button: *(Baton)*
	Knobs: *(Nabs)*
Brasa:	Broil: *(Broil)*
Caliente:	Hot: *(Jat)*
Calor/calefacción:	Heat: *(Jit)*
Cancelar:	Cancel: *(Kensel)*
Cocinar:	Cook: *(Kuk)*
Cordón Eléctrico:	Electric cord: *(Electric cord)*
Corriente:	Power: *(Pawuer)*
Cubos:	Cubes: *(Kiubs)*
Delicado:	Gentle: *(Llentel)*
	Delicate: *(Delikeit)*
Descongelar:	Defrost: *(Difrost)*
Despacio:	Slow: *(Eslou)*
Electricidad:	Electricity: *(Electrisiti)*
Empezar:	Start: *(Estart)*
Empujar:	Push: *(Push)*
Enchufe:	Plug: *(Plag)*
Energía:	Energy: *(Enerlli)*
Enjuagar:	Rinse: *(Rins)*
Frío:	Cold: *(Cold)*
Frío:	Cool: *(Kul)*
Grande:	Large: *(Larch)*
Hornear:	Bake: *(Beik)*

Húmedo:	Damp: *(Demp)*
Jalar:	Pull: *(Pul)*
Limpiar:	Clean: *(Klin)*
Liviano:	Light: *(Lait)*
Luz:	Light: *(Lait)*
Marcador:	Dial: *(Daiel)*
Medio/mediano:	Medium: *(Midium)*
Nivel:	Level: *(Level)*
Parar:	Stop: *(Estop)*
Pausa:	Pause: *(Pous)*
Pequeño:	Small: *(Smol)*
Pesado:	Heavy: *(Jevi)*
Pila/bateria:	Battery: *(Bateri)*
Planchado permanente:	Permanent press: *(Permanent press)*
Prender:	On: *(On)*
Rápido:	Fast: *(Fast)*
Recalentar:	Reheat: *(Rijit)*
Regular:	Regular: *(Regiular)*
Remojar:	Soak: *(Souk)*
Retroseder:	Reverse: *(Rivers)*
Seco:	Dry: *(Drai)*
Taza:	Cup: *(Kap)*
Temperatura:	Temperature: *(Temperachur)*
Tibio:	Warm: *(Worm)*
Tiempo/hora:	Time: *(Taim)*
Tierra:	Soil: *(Soil)*
Tono:	Tuning: *(Tunin)*
Tostar:	Toast: *(Toust)*
Vapor:	Steam: *(Stim)*
Velocidad:	Speed: *(Spid)*
Volumen:	Volume: *(Valium)*

Switches for electric appliances
(Suitches for electric aplaienses)
Artefactos eléctricos suiches

Auto: *(Oto)* Automatic: *(Automatic)*

Automático:

Bake: *(Beik)*   Hornear:

Battery: *(Bateri)*   Pila/batería:

Broil: *(Broil)*   Brasa:

Button: *(Baton)*Knobs: *(Nabs)*   Botón:

Cancel: *(Kensel)*   Cancelar:

Clean: *(Klin)*   Limpiar:

Cold: *(Cold)*   Frío:

Cook: *(Kuk)*   Cocinar:

Cool: *(Kul)*   Frío:

Cubes: *(Kiubs)*   Cubos:

Cup: *(Kap)*   Taza:

Damp: *(Demp)*   Húmedo:

Defrost: *(Difrost)*   Descongelar:

Dial: *(Daiel)*   Marcador:

Dry: *(Drai)*   Seco:

Electric cord: *(Electric cord)*   Cordón eléctrico:

Electricity: *(Electrisiti)*   Electricidad:

Energy: *(Enerlii)*   Energía:

Erase: *(Ireis)*   Borrar:

Fast: *(Fast)*   Rápido:

Forward: *(Fowuar)*   Adelantar:

Gentle: *(Llentel)*Delicate: *(Delikeit)*

Delicado:

Heat: *(Jit)*   Calor/calefacción:

Heavy: *(Jevi)*   Pesado:

High: *(Jai)*   Alto:

Hot: *(Jat)*   Caliente:

Large: *(Larch)*   Grande:

Level: *(Level)*	Nivel:
Light: *(Lait)*	Liviano:
Light: *(Lait)*	Luz:
Low: *(Lou)*	Bajo:
Medium: *(Midium)*	Medio/mediano:
Off: *(Of)*	Apagar:
On: *(On)*	Prender:
Pause: *(Pous)*	Pausa:
Permanent press: *(Permanent press)*	
	Planchado permanente:
Plug: *(Plag)*	Enchufe:
Power: *(Pawuer)*	Corriente:
Pull: *(Pul)*	Jalar:
Push: *(Push)*	Empujar:
Regular: *(Regiular)*	Regular:
Reheat: *(Rijit)*	Recalentar:
Reverse: *(Rivers)*	Retroseder:
Rinse: *(Rins)*	Enjuagar:
Slow: *(Eslou)*	Despacio:
Small: *(Smol)*	Pequeño:
Soak: *(Souk)*	Remojar:
Soil: *(Soil)*	Tierra:
Speed: *(Spid)*	Velocidad:
Start: *(Estart)*	Empezar:
Steam: *(Stim)*	Vapor:
Stop: *(Estop)*	Parar:
Temperature: *(Temperachur)*	Temperatura:
Time: *(Taim)*	Tiempo/hora:
Toast: *(Toust)*	Tostar:
Tuning: *(Tunin)*	Tono:
Volume: *(Valium)*	Volumen:
Warm: *(Worm)*	Tibio:

Tipos de telas
Types of material/fabrics
(Taips of matiriol/fabrics)

Acrílico:	*Acrylic: (Akrilic)*
Algodón:	*Cotton: (Katon)*
Bordado:	*Lace: (Leis)*
Cuero:	*Leather: (Leder)*
Encaje:	*Lace: (Leis)*
Gabardina:	*Gabardine: (Gabardin)*
Gamuza:	*Suede: (Sueid)*
Lana:	*Wool: (Wul)*
Lino:	*Linen: (Linen)*
Lona:	*Canvas: (Kenves)*
Metal:	*Metal: (Metol)*
Mezclilla:	*Denim: (Denim)*
Nailon:	*Nylon: (Nailon)*
Pana:	*Corduroy: (Corduroi)*
Plástico:	*Plastic: (Plastic)*
Poliester:	*Polyester: (Poliester)*
Raso:	*Satin: (Satin)*
Rayón:	*Rayon: (Rellon)*
Satén:	*Satin: (Satin)*
Seda:	*Silk: (Silk)*
Tejidos:	*Knits: (Kenits)*
Terciopelo:	*Velvet: (Velvet)*

Types of material/fabrics
(Taips of matiriol/fabrics)
Tipos de telas

Acrylic: *(Akrilic)*	Acrílico:
Canvas: *(Kenves)*	Lona:
Corduroy: *(Corduroi)*	Pana:
Cotton: *(Katon)*	Algodón:
Denim: *(Denim)*	Mezclilla:
Gabardine: *(Gabardin)*	Gabardina:
Knits: *(Kenits)*	Tejidos:
Lace: *(Leis)*	Bordado:
Lace: *(Leis)*	Encaje:
Leather: *(Leder)*	Cuero:
Linen: *(Linen)*	Lino:
Metal: *(Metol)*	Metal:
Nylon: *(Nailon)*	Nailon:
Plastic: *(Plastic)*	Plástico:
Polyester: *(Poliester)*	Poliester:
Rayon: *(Reilon)*	Rayón:
Satin: *(Satin)*	Raso:
Satin: *(Satin)*	Satén:
Silk: *(Silk)*	Seda:
Suede: *(Sueid)*	Gamuza:
Velvet: *(Velvet)*	Terciopelo:
Wool: *(Wul)*	Lana:

Cosas que hacen los niños
Things that children do
(Sins dat children du)

Bailar:	*Dance: (Dens)*
Bañar:	*Bathe: (Beis)*
Besar:	*Kiss: (Kis)*
Caminar:	*Walk: (Wok)*
Cantar:	*Sing: (Sing)*
Dibujar:	*Draw: (Dro)*
Dormir:	*Sleep: (Slip)*
Escribir:	*Write: (Rait)*
Estudiar:	*Study: (Stadi)*
Gatear:	*Crawl: (Croul)*
Gritar:	*Scream: (Skrim)*
Hablar:	*Talk: (Tok)*
Jugar:	*Play: (Plei)*
Leer:	*Read: (Rid)*
Llorar:	*Cry: (Crai)*
Manejar Bicicleta:	*Ride a bike: (Raid el baik)*
Mentir:	*Lie: (Lai)*
Nadar:	*Swim: (Suim)*
Pelear:	*Fight: (Fait)*
Pintar:	*Paint: (Peint)*
Reir:	*Laugh: (Laf)*
Rompecabezas:	*Puzzles: (Pazels)*
Verdad:	*True: (Tru)*
Otras cosas:	*Other:*

Things that children do
(Sins dat children du)
Cosas que hacen los niños

Bathe: *(Beis)*	Bañar:
Crawl: *(Croul)*	Gatear:
Cry: *(Crai)*	Llorar:
Dance: *(Dens)*	Bailar:
Draw: *(Dro)*	Dibujar:
Fight: *(Fait)*	Pelear:
Kiss: *(Kis)*	Besar:
Laugh: *(Laf)*	Reir:
Lie: *(Lai)*	Mentir:
Paint: *(Peint)*	Pintar:
Play: *(Plei)*	Jugar:
Puzzles: *(Pazels)*	Rompecabezas:
Read: *(Rid)*	Leer:
Ride a bike: *(Raid ei baik)*	Manejar Bicicleta:
Scream: *(Skrim)*	Gritar:
Sing: *(Sing)*	Cantar:
Sleep: *(Slip)*	Dormir:
Study: *(Stadi)*	Estudiar:
Swim: *(Suim)*	Nadar:
Talk: *(Tok)*	Hablar:
True: *(Tru)*	Verdad:
Walk: *(Wok)*	Caminar:
Write: *(Rait)*	Escribir:
Other: *(Ader)*	Otras Cosas:

Cosas del bebé
Baby things
(Beibi sings)

Aceite de bebé:	Baby oil: *(Beibi oil)*
Andadera:	Walker: *(Wuoker)*
Baberos:	Bibs: *(Bibs)*
Bañerita:	Bath tub: *(Bas tab)*
Caja de arena:	Sand box: *(Send box)*
Caja de música:	Music box: *(Miusic bax)*
Calentador de botellas:	Bottle warmer: *(Batel wormer)*
Calzones para entrenar:	Training pants: *(Treinin pents)*
Calzón de plástico:	Weatherproof/plastic pants:
	(Plastic pents)
Canasta:	Bassinette: *(Basinet)*
Cascabel/maraca/sonaja:	Rattle: *(Ratel)*
Cepillo suave de pelo:	Soft hair brush: *(Soft jer brash)*
Cereal:	Cereal: *(Sirial)*
Chupón/chupete:	Pacifier: *(Pasifaier)*
Cobija:	Blanket: *(Blanket)*
Coche/Carrola:	Stroller: *(Stroler)*
Columpio:	Swing: *(Suin)*
Compota:	Baby food: *(Beibi fud)*
Corral:	Playpen: *(Pleipen)*
Cómoda:	Chest of drawers: *(Chest of*
	drous)
Crema:	Cream: *(Krim)*
Cuna:	Crib: *(Krib)*
Dormilona/pijama:	Sleeper: *(Sliper)*
Escarpines:	Booties: *(Butis)*
Esterilizador:	Sterilizer: *(Sterilaiser)*
Imperdibles/gancho de seguro:	Safety pins: *(Seifti pins)*
Jabón:	Soap: *(Soup)*
Juguete:	Toys: *(Tois)*

Litera:	*Bunk bed:* **(Bank bed)**
Lonchera:	*Lunch box:* **(Lanch box)**
Mesedora:	*Rocking chair.* **(Rakin cher)**
Mobil:	*Mobile:* **(Mobil)**
Muñeca:	*Doll:* **(Dol)**
Overoles:	*Overalls:* **(Overols)**
Pañalera:	*Diaper bag:* **(Diaper bag)**
Pañales:	*Diapers:* **(Daipers)**
Porta bebé:	*Baby carrier.* **(Beibi karrier)**
Ropero/canasta ropa sucia:	*Hamper.* **(Jemper)**
Salpullido:	*Rash:* **(Rash)**
Salvavidas:	*Life jacket:* **(Laif yaket)**
Shampú de bebé:	*Baby shampoo:* **(Beibi shampu)**
Silla de carro:	*Car seat.* **(Car sit)**
Silla de comer:	*High chair.* **(Jai cher)**
Silla de entrenar:	*Training seat.* **(Treinin sit)**
Talco de bebé:	*Baby powder.* **(Beibi pauder)**
Tetero/biberón/pacha/botella:	*Bottle:* **(Batel)**
Tira pañales/Dispensa de pañales:	*Diaper pail:* **(Daiper peil)**
Toalla:	*Towel:* **(Tawuel)**
Toallas mojadas:	*Wet wipes:* **(Wet waips)**
Tobogán:	*Slide:* **(Slaid)**
Vestidor/cambiador:	*Dressing table:* **(Dresin teibel)**

Conversation: Expressions
(Converseishon: Expreshons)
Conversación: Expresiones

Here are some words that will help you with the next pages.
Aquí hay algunas palabras que le ayudarán para las páginas siguientes.

NOTE: *Throughout this book, when possible, I have used contractions to help the Spanish speaking person use both the long and abbreviated words. (Eg. "You're" instead of "you are").*

Bad: *(Bed)*	Malo:
Breakfast: *(Brekfast)*	Desayuno:
Clean: *(Klin)*	Limpio:
Cold: *(Cold)*	Frío:
Dinner: *(Diner)*	Cena:
Dirty: *(Derti)*	Sucio:
Down: *(Daun)*	Abajo:
Empty: *(Empti)*	Vacio:
Everything: *(Evrising)*	Todo:
Fat: *(Fat)*	Gordo:
Few: *(Fiu)*	Poco:
Finish: *(Finish)*	Terminar:
Full: *(Ful)*	Lleno:
Good: *(Gud)*	Bueno:
Here: *(Jir)*	Aquí:
Hot: *(Jat)*	Caliente:
In the middle: *(In di midel)*	En el medio:
Inside/in: *(Insaid/in)*	Adentro:
Is here: *(Is jir)*	Esta:
Is not here: *(Is nat jir)*	No está:
Less: *(Les)*	Menos:
Lunch: *(Lanch)*	Almuerzo/lonche:

Many times: *(**Meni taims**)*	Muchas Veces:
More or less: *(**Mor or les**)*	Más o Menos:
More: *(**Mor**)*	Más:
Much: *(**Mach**)*	Mucho:
Never: *(**Never**)*	Nunca:
Next day: *(**Next dei**)*	El día siguiente:
No: *(**Nou**)*	No:
Nothing: *(**Nasin**)*	Nada:
Now: *(**Nau**)*	Ahora:
Outside/out: *(**Autsaid/aut**)*	Afuera:
Short: *(**Short**)*	Bajo (estatura):
Skinny: *(**Skini**)*	Flaco:
Snack: *(**Snak**)*	Merienda:
Start: *(**Start**)*	Empezar:
Tol: *(**Tol**)*	Alto (estatura):
The (Feminine): *(**Di**)* Las (plural)	La:
The (Masculine): *(**Di**)* Los (plural)	El:
There: *(**Der**)*	Allá:
Today: *(**Tudei**)*	Hoy:
Tomorrow: *(**Tumorou**)*	Mañana:
Up:	Arriba:
Warm: *(**orm**)*	Tibio:
Yes:	Si:
Yesterday: *(**Yesterdei**)*	Ayer:
Have you? *(**Jev yu**)*	Tiene Usted?
How much? *(**Jau mach**)*	Cuánto?
How? *(**Jau**)*	Cómo?
What? *(**Wuat**)*	Qué?
When? *(**Wuen**)*	Cuándo?
Where is? *(**Wuer is**)*	Dónde está?
Which one? *(**Wuich wan**)*	Cuál?
Who? *(**Ju**)*	Quién?
Why? *(**Wuai**)*	Por qué?

I hope so: **(Ai jop sou)**   Espero que si:

I think so: **(Ai sink sou)**   Creo que si:

Not yet: **(Nat yet)**   Todavía no:

Conversación de Cocina
Kitchen Conversation
(Kitchen Converseishon)

1. Tienes hambre?
   Are you hungry?
   (Ar yu jangri?)

2. Tienes sed?
   Are you thirsty?
   (Ar yu sersti?)

3. Quieres algo de comer?
   Do you want something to eat?
   (Du yu want somsin tu it?)

4. Quieres algo de tomar?
   Do you want something to drink?
   (Du yu want somsin tu drink?)

5. Vamos tener visita para comer?
   Are we having company for _____?
   (Ar wi jevin compani for _____?)

6. Ayúdame a cocinar.
   Help me cook.
   (Jelp mi kuk.)

7. Tenemos que comprar _____.
   We need to buy _____.
   (Wi nid to buy _____.)

8. No tenemos más _____.
   We don't have any _____.
   (Wi dont jev eni _____.)

9. La comida está lista.
   The food is ready.
   (Di fud is redi.)

10. Quieres una merienda?
    Do you want a snack?
    (Du yu want ei snak?)

11. Te gusta ?
Do you like it?
(Du yu laik et?)

12. Me puedes pasar _____ por favor!
Can you pass me the _____ please!
(Ken yu pas mi di _____ plis!)

13. La/el _____ no trabaja/sirve.
The _____ is not working.
(Di _____ is nat wuorkin.)

14. La comida está _____.
The food is _____.
(Di fud is _____.)

15. Cuidado que no se queme.
Careful, do not get burned.
(Kerful, du nat get bern.)

16. Tenemos que lavar _____.
We need to wash the _____.
(Wi nid tu wash di _____.)

17. Tápe la comida en la nevera.
Cover the food in the refrigerator.
(Kaver di fud in di refrillireitor.)

18. Déjeme ayudar.
Let me help you.
(Let mi jelp yu.)

19. Guarde los comestibles en su lugar.
Put the groceries away.
(Put di groceris owai.)

20. Póngalo por _____.
Put it _____.
(Put it _____.)

21. Un poco _____.
A little _____.
(E litel _____.)

22. Ten cuidado con _____.
    Be careful with the _____.
    (BI kerful wis di _____.)
23. Vacíe el/la _____.
    Empty the _____.
    (Empti di _____.)
24. Sirva _____ por favor!
    Serve the _____ please!
    (Serv di _____ plis!)
25. Vamos a comer _____.
    We will eat _____.
    (Wi wil it _____.)
26. Cómo lo quiere?
    How do you want it?
    (Jau du yu wuant it?)
27. Qué tiene para postre?
    What is for dessert?
    (Wuat is for desert?)
28. Tiene la receta.
    Do you have the recipe?
    (Du yu jev di resepi?)
29. Estás a dieta?
    Are you on a diet?
    (Ar yu on ei daiet?)

Conversación de Baño
Bathroom Conversation
(Basrum Converseishon)

1. Bañarse en la bañera o ducha.
   Take a bath or a shower.
   (Teik ei bas or ei shawer.)

2. Necesita _____?
   Do you need _____?
   (Du yu nid _____?)

3. El agua está muy _____.
   The water is too _____.
   (Di water is tu _____.)

4. El exusado está roto.
   The toilet is broken.
   (Di toilet is brouken.)

5. No hay agua _____.
   There is not _____ water.
   (Der is nat _____ water.)

6. El/la _____ está _____.
   The _____ is_____.
   (Di _____ is _____.)

7. Se va a lavar el pelo?
   Are you washing your hair?
   (Ar yu washin yor jer?)

8. Cepíllece el/los _____.
   Brush your _____.
   (Brash yor _____.)

9. Córtece _____.
   Cut your _____.
   (Kat yor _____.)

10. Huele muy _____.
    Smells too _____.
    (Smels tu _____.)

11. Está tomando mucho tiempo.
    It is taking too long.
    (It Is teikin tu long.)
12. No desperdicie el agua.
    Don't waste water.
    (Dont weist water.)
13. Reemplace el papel.
    Replace the paper.
    (Ripleis di peiper.)
14. Tengo que usar el baño.
    I have to use the bathroom.
    (Ai jev tu yus di basrum.)
15. Cierra/abra la puerta.
    Close/Open the door.
    (Clous/oupen di dor.)
16. El _____ está mojado.
    The _____ is wet.
    (Di _____ is wet.)
17. El basurero está lleno.
    The trash can is full.
    (Di trash ken is ful.)
18. No trabaja/funciona.
    It's not working.
    (its nat wourking.)
19. Limpie _____.
    Wipe _____.
    (Waip di _____.)
20. Friegue _____.
    Scrub the _____.
    (Scrab di _____.)
21. Rocíe el esprai _____.
    Spray the _____.
    (Esprei di _____.)

22. Cambie las toallas.
    Change the towel.
    (Cheinch di tawel.)
23. Baje el agua del excusado.
    Flush the toilet.
    (Flash di toilet.)
24. Aquí hay moho.
    There is some mildew here.
    (Der is som meldiu jir.)
25. Qué necesita?
    What do you need?
    (Wuat du yu nid?)

Conversación de Limpieza
Cleaning Conversation
(Clinin Converseishon)

El cuestionario también le ayudará para este tema!
The questionnaire will help for this subject too!

1. Separe la ropa antes de lavar.
   Sort the clothes before washing.
   (Sourt di clous bifor washin.)

2. Por favor limpie _____.
   Please clean the _____.
   (Plis clin di _____.)

3. Quite la ropa de _____.
   Remove the clothes from _____.
   (Rimuv clous from _____.)

4. Friegue la _____ por favor.
   Please scrub the _____.
   (Plis scrab di _____.)

5. Recoga el _____.
   Pick up the _____.
   (Pik ap di _____.)

6. Lave este _____ a mano.
   Wash this _____ by hand.
   (Wuash dis _____ bai jend.)

7. No ponga este _____ en la secodora.
   Do not put this _____ in the dryer.
   (Du not put dis _____ in di drayer.)

8. La lavadora está _____.
   The dishwasher is _____.
   (Di dishwasher is _____.)

9. Puede recoger la mesa.
   You can pick up the _____ table.
   (Yu ken pik ap di _____ teibol.)

10. Cepille el _____ por favor.
    Brush the _____ please.
    (Brash di _____ plis.)
11. Doble las _____.
    Fold the _____.
    (Fold di _____.)
12. Arregle los _____.
    Arrange the _____.
    (Arreinch di _____.)
13. Cuelgue el _____.
    Hang up the _____.
    (Jeng ap di _____.)
14. Tienda la cama.
    Make the bed.
    (Meik di bed.)
15. Puede coserme esta _____.
    Can you sew this _____.
    (Ken yu sou dis _____.)
16. Lustre estos zapatos.
    Shine these shoes.
    (Shain dis shus.)

Conversación Social
Social Conversation
(Soshol Converseishon)

This part may also help to answer the telephone.

A la order:	You're welcome: *(Yur welcom)*
Adiós:	Goodbye: *(Gudbai)*
Aniversario:	Anniversary: *(Aniversari)*
Bien, gracias:	Fine, thank you: *(Fain, tenkiu)*
Bonita:	Pretty: *(Priti)*
Buen provecho:	Enjoy your meal: *(Enlloi yor mil)*
Buena suerte:	Good luck: *(Gud lak)*
Buenos días:	Good morning: *(Gud Mornin)*
Buenas noches:	Good night: *(Gud nait)*
Buenas tardes:	Good afternoon: *(Gud afternun)*
Cómo estás?:	How are you?: *(Jau ar yu?)*
Cómo se llama?:	What's your name?: *(Wuats yur neim?)*
Cómo te sientes?:	How are you feeling?: *(Jau ar yu filin?)*
Cuánto cuesta?:	How much is it?: *(Jau mach is it?)*
Cumpleaños:	Birthday: *(Berdei)*
De nada:	You're welcome: *(Yur welcom)*
Déle mis saludos:	Send my regards: *(Send mai rigards)*
Depende de ti:	It is up to you: *(It is ap tu yu)*
Déjeme tomar su abrigo:	Let me take your coat: *(Let mi teik yor cout)*
Disculpe:	I apologize: *(Ai apoloyais)*
Duerma bien:	Sleep well: *(Slip wuel)*
Encantado en conocerle:	Nice to meet you: *(Nais tu mit yu)*

Enfermo:	Sick: *(Sik)*
Entre por favor:	Come in, please: *(Kam in plis)*
Escúseme:	Excuse me: *(Exus mi)*
Eso es:	That's it: *(Dats it)*
Espere aquí:	Wait here: *(Weit jir)*
Estás _____ ?:	Are you _____ ?: *(Ar yu _____ ?)*
Estoy esperando un paquete:	I'm expecting a package: *(Ayam expectin ei pakech)*
Fea:	Ugly: *(Agli)*
Felicidades:	Congratulations: *(Congratuleishons)*
Felíz:	Happy: *(Japi)*
Fiesta:	Holiday: *(Jolidei)*
Gracias:	Thank you: *(Tenkiu)*
Hasta luego:	See you later: *(Si yu leiter)*
Hola:	Hi/Hello: *(Jai/Jelou)*
Lo siento:	I'm sorry: *(Ayam sorri)*
Más o menos:	So so: *(So sou)*
Me gustaría _____:	I would like _____: *(Ai wud laik _____)*
Me iré mañana:	I will leave tomorrow: *(Ai wil liv tumorrou)*
Me permite?:	Do you mind?: *(Du yu maind?)*
Me siento mal:	I feel sick: *(Ai fil sik)*
Mi nombre es _____.:	My name is _____.: *(Mai neim is _____.)*
Muy caro:	Very expensive: *(Veri expensiv)*
Necesito salir temprano, puede ser posible?:	I need to leave early, could it be possible?: *(Ai nid tu liv erli, cud it bi pasebol?)*
Necesito ver a un médico:	I need to see a doctor: *(Ai nid tu si ei dactor)*
No lo sabía:	I did not know: *(Ai did not nou)*

No muy bien:	*Not so good:* **(Nat so gud)**
Okei:	*O.K.:* **(Okei)**
Perdí dinero:	*I have lost money:* **(Ai jev lost mani)**
Perdóneme:	*Excuse me:* **(Ex-kius mi)**
Por favor:	*Please:* **(Plis)**
Puedo ayudarlo en algo?:	*May I help you?:* **(Mei ai jelp yu?)**
Que goces:	*Have fun:* **(Jev fan)**
Qué hay de nuevo?:	*What's new?:* **(Wuats niu?)**
Qué hora es?:	*What time is it?:* **(Wuat taim is it?)**
Qué tiene de malo?:	*What is wrong about it?:* **(Wuat is rong abaut it?)**
Quiere oir música?:	*Do you want to listen to the music?:* **(Du yu wuant tu lisen tu di miusic?)**
Quiere ver televisión?:	*Do you want to watch T.V.?:* **(Du yu wuant tu wach TiVi?)**
Quién llamó?:	*Who called?:* **(Ju koled?)**
Quién vino?:	*Who came over?:* **(Ju keim over?)**
Salud (estornudo):	*Bless you (When you sneeze):* **(Bles yu)**
Se ve bien:	*You look good:* **(Yu luk gud)**
Siéntese aquí:	*Sit here:* **(Sit jir)**
Siento haber llegado tarde:	*I am sorry I am late:* **(Ayam sorri ayam leit)**
Sólo:	*Lonely:* **(Lonli)**
Te quiero:	*I love you:* **(Ai lov yu)**
Tenga un buen día:	*Have a nice day:* **(Jev ei nais dei)**
Tengo algún mensaje?:	*Do I have any messages?:* **(Du ai jev eni mesalles?)**

Tengo muchas cosas que hacer:	*I have many things to do:* **(Ai jev meni sings tu du)**
Tengo una cita:	*I have an appointment:* **(Ai jev en apointment)**
Tiene calor?:	*Are you hot?:* **(Ar yu jat?)**
Tiene fiebre?:	*Do you have a fever?:* **(Du yu jev ei fiver?)**
Tiene frío?:	*Are you cold?:* **(Ar yu cold?)**
Triste:	*Sad:* **(Sad)**
Voy a estar en este teléfono:	*I'm going to be at this phone number:* **(Ayam goin tu bi at dis fon namber)**
Yo estoy contento:	*I am happy:* **(Ayam japi)**
Yo voy a _____.:	*I'm going to the _____.:* **(Ayam goin tu di _____.)**

Social Conversation
(Soshol Converseishon)
Conversación Social

This part may also help to answer the telephone.

Anniversary: *(Aniversari)*   Aniversario:

Are you cold?: *(Ar yu cold?)*   Tiene frío?:

Are you hot?: *(Ar yu jat?)*   Tiene calor?:

Are you _____ *?*: *(Ar yu_____ ?)*

                Estás _____ ?:

Birthday: *(Berdei)*   Cumpleaños:

Bless you (When you sneeze): *(Bles yu)*

                Salud (estornudo):

Come in, please: *(Kam in plis)*   Entre por favor:

Congratulations: *(Congratuleishons)*

                Felicidades:

Do I have any messages?: *(Du ai jev eni mesalles?)*

                Tengo algún mensaje?:

Do you have a fever?: *(Du yu jev ei fiver?)*

                Tiene fiebre?:

Do you mind?: *(Du yu maind?)*   Me permite?:

Do you want to listen to the music?: *(Du yu wuant tu lisen tu di miusic?)*

                Quiere oir música?:

Do you want to watch T.V.?: *(Du yu wuant tu wach TiVi?)*

                Quiere ver television?:

Enjoy your meal: *(Enlloi yor mil)*   Buen provecho:

Excuse me: *(Ex-kius mi)*   Perdóneme:

Excuse me: *(Exus mi)*   Escúseme:

Fine, thank you: *(Fain, tenkiu)*   Bien, gracias:

Good afternoon: *(Gud afternun)*   Buenas tardes:

Good luck: *(Gud lak)*   Buena suerte:

Good morning: *(Gud Mornin)*   Buenos días:

Good night: *(Gud nait)*   Buenas noches:

Goodbye: *(Gudbai)*   Adiós:

Happy: *(Japi)*   Felíz:

Have a nice day: *(Jev ei nais dei)* Tenga un buen día:

Have fun: *(Jev fan)*   Que goces:

Hi/Hello: *(Jai/Jelou)*   Hola:

Holiday: *(Jolidei)*   Fiesta:

How are you feeling?: *(Jau ar yu filin?)*

     Cómo te sientes?:

How are you?: *(Jau ar yu?)*   Cómo estás?:

How much is it?: *(Jau mach is it?)* Cuánto cuesta?:

I am happy: *(Ayam japi)*   Yo estoy contento:

I am sorry I am late: *(Ayam sorri ayam leit)*

     Siento haber llegado tarde:

I apologize: *(Ai apoloyais)*   Disculpe:

I did not know: *(Ai did not nou)* No lo sabía:

I feel sick: *(Ai fil sik)*   Me siento mal:

I have an appointment: *(Ai jev en apointment)*

     Tengo una cita:

I have lost money: *(Ai jev lost mani)*

     Perdí dinero:

I have many things to do: *(Ai jev meni sings tu du)*

     Tengo muchas cosas que hacer:

I love you: *(Ai lov yu)*   Te quiero:

I need to leave early, could it be possible?: *(Ai nid tu liv erli, cud it*

     bi pasebol?)

     Necesito salir temprano, puede ser

     posible?:

I need to see a doctor: *(Ai nid tu si ei dactor)*

     Necesito ver a un médico:

I will leave tomorrow: *(Ai wil liv tumorrou)*

     Me iré mañana:

I would like _to_: *(Ai wud laik _see_)*

     Me gustaría _you_ :

I'm expecting a package: *(Ayam expectin ei pakech)*
Estoy esperando un paquete:

I'm going to be at this phone number: *(Ayam goin tu bi at dis fon namber)*
Voy a estar en este teléfono:

I'm going to the _____.: *(Ayam goin tu di _____.)*
Yo voy a _____.:

I'm sorry: *(Ayam sorri)* — Lo siento:

It is up to you: *(Et is ap tu yu)* — Depende de ti:

Let me take your coat: *(Let mi teik yor cout)*
Déjeme tomar su abrigo:

Lonely: *(Lonli)* — Sólo:

May I help you?: *(Mei ai jelp yu?)* — Puedo ayudarlo en algo?:

My name is _____.: *(Mai neim is _____.)*
Mi nombre es _____.:

Nice to meet you: *(Nais tu mit yu)*
Encantado en conocerle:

Not so good: *(Nat so gud)* — No muy bien:

O.K.: *(Okei)* — Okei:

Please: *(Plis)* — Por favor:

Pretty: *(Priti)* — Bonita:

Sad: *(Sad)* — Triste:

See you later: *(Si yu leiter)* — Hasta luego:

Send my regards: *(Send mai rigards)*
Déle mis saludos:

Sick: *(Sik)* — Enfermo:

Sit here: *(Sit jir)* — Siéntese aquí:

Sleep well: *(Slip wuel)* — Duerma bien:

So so: *(So sou)* — Más o menos:

Thank you: *(Tenkiu)* — Gracias:

That's it: *(Dats it)* — Eso es:

Ugly: *(Agli)* — Fea:

Very expensive: *(Veri expensiv)* — Muy caro:

Wait here: *(Weit jir)* — Espere aquí:

What is wrong about it?: (Wuat is rong abaut it?)

Qué tiene de malo?:

What time is it?: (Wuat taim is it?) Qué hora es?:

What's new?: (Wuats niu?) Qué hay de nuevo?:

What's your name?: (Wuats yur neim)

Cómo se llama?:

Who called?: (Ju koled?) Quién llamó?:

Who came over?: (Ju keim over?) Quién vino?:

You look good: (Yu luk gud) Se ve bien:

You're welcome: (Yur welcom) A la order:

You're welcome: (Yur welcom) De nada:

Conversación del Cuidado de Niños
Children Care Conversation
(Children Ker Converseishon)

Esta parte también lo ayudará para expresarse socialmente.
This part will also help you for social expressions.

Cuídame al niño:

Take care of the child: *(Teik ker of di chaild)*

Ayúdale a vestirse:

Help him get dressed: *(Jelp jim get dres)*

Pónlo a dormir:

Put her to sleep: *(Put ier tu slip)*

No puede comer esto:

He can't eat this: *(Ji kent it dis)*

Juege con el niño:

Play with the child: *(Plei wuis di chaild)*

Cuidado con las cosas pequeñas que no se las meta en la boca:

Be careful with the little items so he doesn't put them in his mouth: *(Bi kerful wis di litel aitems sou ji dasent put dem in jis maus.)*

El niño va a casa de un amigo:

The child is going to a friends house: *(Di chaild is going tu el frends jaus)*

No le grite o pegue al niño:

Do not scream or spank the child: *(Du nat scrim or spenk di chaild)*

La niña está castiga:

The girl is punished: *(Di gerl is panish)*

Por favor, pórtese bien:

Please behave well: *(Plis bijeiv wel)*

Le voy a decir a tus padres:

I am going to tell your parents: *(Ayam going tu tel yor perents)*

No tengas miedo:	*Do not be afraid:* **(Du nat bi efreid)**
No llores:	*Don't cry:* **(Dont crai)**
Quieres que te ayude?:	*Do you want me to help you?:* **(Du yu wuant mi tu jelp yu?)**
No puedes:	*You can't:* **(Yu kent)**
Recoge los juguetes:	*Pick up the toys:* **(Pik ap di tois)**
Estás bien?:	*Are you O.K.?:* **(Ar yu okei?)**
Qué te duele?:	*What hurts?:* **(Wuat jerts?)**
Tienes frío?:	*Are you cold?:* **(Ar yu cold?)**
Cómo te fué hoy?:	*How did it go today?:* **(Jau did it gou tudei?)**
Tienes que hacer la tarea ahora:	*You have to do your homework now:* **(Yu jev tu du yor jomwuork nau)**
Llama a tu <u>mamá</u> primero:	*Call your <u>mom</u> first:* **(Kol yor <u>mam</u> ferst)**
Tienes permiso?	*Do you have permission?:* **(Du yu jev permishion?)**
No haga eso:	*Do not do that:* **(Du nat du dat)**
A dónde vas?:	*Where are you going?:* **(Wuer ar yu going?)**
Vamos a comer:	*Let's eat:* **(Lets it)**
Qué comió?:	*What did <u>he</u> eat?:* **(Wuat did <u>ji</u> it?)**
Que lindo!:	*How pretty!:* **(Jau priti!)**
Quieres leer libros?:	*Do you want to read a book?:* **(Du yu wuant tu rid ei buk?)**
No puede llegar tarde:	*You can't come late:* **(Yu kent kam leit)**
Qué pasó?:	*What happened?:* **(Wuat Japen?)**
No peleen:	*Do not fight:* **(Du nat fait)**
Estoy tan orgullosa de ti:	*I am so proud of you:* **(Ayam sou praud of yu)**

Qué necesitas?:	What do you need?: (*Wuat du yu nid?*)
El niño es alérgico a la <u>leche</u>:	The child is allergic to <u>milk</u>: (*Di chaild is alerllic tu <u>milk</u>*)
Cállense por favor:	Be quiet please: (*Bi kuayet plis*)
Me pica:	It itches: (*It iches*)
Cuidado por donde caminas:	Watch your step: (*Wuach yor step*)
No quiero problemas:	I don't want any trouble: (*Ai dont wuant eni trabol*)
No seas tonto:	Don't be silly: (*Dont bi sill*)
No te preocupes:	Don't worry: (*Dont wuorri*)
Cómo es posible?:	How come?: (*Jau com?*)
Qué lastima:	What a pity: (*Wuat e piti*)
Estoy bromeando:	I am kidding: (*Ayam kidin*)
Sin resentimientos:	No hard feelings: (*No jard filins*)
Tómalo con calma:	Take it easy: (*Teik it isi*)
Me estoy volviendo loco:	I am going crazy: (*Ayam goin kreisi*)
Debes avergonzarte:	Shame on you: (*Sheim on yu*)
Por el amor de dios:	For heavens sake: (*For jevens seik*)
Me gusta mucho:	I like it a lot: (*Ai laik it e lat*)
Para qué es eso?:	What is that for? (*Wuat is dat for?*)
Vamos _____:	Come on _____, let's go: (*Cam on _____, lets gou*)

Partes del Cuerpo Humano
Parts of the Human Body
(Parts of di Jiuman Badi)

Cabeza:	Head: *(Jed)*
Barbilla:	Chin: *(Chin)*
Bigote:	Mustache: *(Mustash)*
Boca:	Mouth: *(Maus)*
Cachetes:	Cheeks: *(Chiks)*
Cara/Rostro:	Face: *(Feis)*
Cejas:	Eyebrow: *(Aibrau)*
Cerebro:	Brain: *(Brein)*
Cuello:	Neck: *(Nek)*
Diente:	Tooth: *(Tus)*
Dientes:	Teeth: *(Tis)*
Frente:	Forehead: *(Forjed)*
Garganta:	Throat: *(Srout)*
Labios:	Lips: *(Lips)*
Lágrimas:	Tears: *(Tirs)*
Lengua:	Tongue: *(Tong)*
Lóbulo del Oído:	Ear Lobe: *(Ir lob)*
Muela:	Molar: *(Moler)*
Naríz:	Nose: *(Nous)*
Oídos:	Ears: *(Iers)*
Ojos:	Eyes: *(Ais)*
Párpado:	Eyelid: *(Ailid)*
Pelo/Cabello:	Hair: *(Jer)*
Pestaña:	Eyelash: *(Ailash)*

Cuerpo:	Body: **(Badi)**
Arruga:	Wrinkle: **(Wrinkel)**
Axila:	Underarm/Armpit: **(Anderarm/Armpit)**
Brazos:	Arms: **(Arms)**
Bronquio:	Bronchia: **(Bronjia)**
Caderas:	Hips: **(Jips)**
Cintura:	Waist: **(Weist)**
Codo:	Elbow: **(Elbou)**
Corazón:	Heart: **(Jart)**
Dedos de la Mano:	Fingers: **(Fingers)**
Dedos de los Pie:	Toes: **(Tous)**
Espalda:	Back: **(Bak)**
Estómago:	Stomach: **(Stomak)**
Grasa:	Fat: **(Fat)**
Hígado:	Liver: **(Liver)**
Hombros:	Shoulders: **(Shoulders)**
Hueso:	Bone: **(Boun)**
Intestino:	Intestine: **(Intestin)**
Lunar:	Mole: **(Mol)**
Manos:	Hands: **(Jends)**
Menstruación:	Period/Menstruation: **(Piriod)**
Muñeca:	Wrist: **(Rist)**
Muslo:	Thigh: **(Sai)**
Músculo:	Muscle: **(Masel)**
Nalgas:	Buttocks/Butt: **(Batoks/Bat)**
Ombligo:	Belly Button: **(Beli Baton)**
Organos Sexuales:	Sexual Organs: **(Sexsual Organs)**
Ovario:	Ovary: **(Ovari)**
Pantorilla:	Calf: **(Calf)**
Peca:	Freckle: **(Frecol)**
Pecho:	Chest: **(Chest)**
Pesón:	Nipple: **(Nipol)**
Pie:	Foot: **(Fut)**

Piel:	*Skin*: **(Skin)**
Piernas:	*Legs*: **(Legs)**
Pies:	*Feet*: **(Fit)**
Pulgar:	*Thumb*: **(Samb)**
Pulmones:	*Lungs*: **(Langs)**
Riñon:	*Kidney*: **(Kidni)**
Rodilla:	*Knee*: **(Nii)**
Sangre:	*Blood*: **(Blad)**
Tendón:	*Tendon*: **(Tendon)**
Tobillo:	*Ankle*: **(Enkel)**
Uñas de Mano:	*Fingernails*: **(Fingerneils)**
Uñas de Pie:	*Toenails*: **(Toneils)**
Utero:	*Uterus*: **(Yuterus)**
Vejiga:	*Bladder*: **(Blader)**
Vellos/Pelo:	*Hair*: **(Jer)**
Venas:	*Veins*: **(Veins)**

Parts of the Human Body
(Parts of di Jiuman Badi)
Partes del Cuerpo Humano

Head: *(Jed)*	Cabeza:
Brain: *(Brein)*	Cerebro:
Cheeks: *(Chiks)*	Cachetes:
Chin: *(Chin)*	Barbilla:
Ear Lobe: *(Ir lob)*	Lóbulo del Oído:
Ears: *(iers)*	Oídos:
Eyebrow: *(Aibrau)*	Cejas:
Eyelash: *(Ailash)*	Pestaña:
Eyelid: *(Ailid)*	Párpado:
Eyes: *(Ais)*	Ojos:
Face: *(Feis)*	Cara/Rostro:
Forehead: *(Forjed)*	Frente:
Hair: *(Jer)*	Pelo/Cabello:
Lips: *(Lips)*	Labios:
Molar: *(Moler)*	Muela:
Mouth: *(Maus)*	Boca:
Mustache: *(Mustash)*	Bigote:
Neck: *(Nek)*	Cuello:
Nose: *(Nous)*	Naríz:
Tears: *(Tirs)*	Lágrimas:
Teeth: *(Tis)*	Dientes:
Throat: *(Srout)*	Garganta:
Tongue: *(Tong)*	Lengua:
Tooth: *(Tus)*	Diente:

Body: **(Badi)**	Cuerpo:
Ankle: **(Enkel)**	Tobillo:
Arms: **(Arms)**	Brazos:
Back: **(Bak)**	Espalda:
Belly Button: **(Beli Baton)**	Ombligo:
Bladder: **(Blader)**	Vejiga:
Blood: **(Blad)**	Sangre:
Bone: **(Boun)**	Hueso:
Bronchia: **(Bronjia)**	Bronquio:
Buttocks/Butt: **(Batoks/Bat)**	Nalgas:
Calf: **(Calf)**	Pantorilla:
Chest: **(Chest)**	Pecho:
Elbow: **(Elbou)**	Codo:
Fat: **(Fat)**	Grasa:
Feet: **(Fit)**	Pies:
Fingernails: **(Fingerneils)**	Uñas de Mano:
Fingers: **(Fingers)**	Dedos de la Mano:
Foot: **(Fut)**	Pie:
Freckle: **(Frecol)**	Peca:
Hair. **(Jer)**	Vellos/Pelo:
Hands: **(Jends)**	Manos:
Heart: **(Jart)**	Corazón:
Hips: **(Jips)**	Caderas:
Intestine: **(Intestin)**	Intestino:
Kidney: **(Kidni)**	Riñon:
Knee: **(Nii)**	Rodilla:
Legs: **(Legs)**	Piernas:
Liver. **(Liver)**	Hígado:
Lungs: **(Langs)**	Pulmones:
Mole: **(Mol)**	Lunar:
Muscle: **(Masel)**	Músculo:
Nipple: **(Nipol)**	Pesón:
Ovary: **(Ovari)**	Ovario:
Period/Menstruation: **(Piriod)**	Menstruación:
Sexual Organs: **(Sexsual Organs)**	Organos Sexuales:

Shoulders: **(Shoulder)**	Hombros:
Skin: **(Skin)**	Piel:
Stomach: **(Stomak)**	Estómago:
Tendon: **(Tendon)**	Tendón:
Thigh: **(Sai)**	Muslo:
Thumb: **(Samb)**	Pulgar:
Toenails: **(Tonells)**	Uñas de Pie:
Toes: **(Tous)**	Dedos de los Pie:
Underarm/Armpit: **(Anderarm/Armpit)**	
	Axila:
Uterus: **(Yuterus)**	Utero:
Veins: **(Veins)**	Venas:
Waist: **(Weist)**	Cintura:
Wrinkle: **(Wrinkel)**	Arruga:
Wrist: **(Rist)**	Muñeca:

Información Médica
Medical Information
(Medikal Informeishon)

Aborto:	Miscarriage: *(Miskerech)*
Abseso:	Abscess: *(Abses)*
Accidente:	Accident: *(Axident)*
Acostado:	Lying down: *(Lain daun)*
Afloje:	Loosen: *(Lusen)*
Ahogado en Agua:	Drowning: *(Draunin)*
Ahogado:	Choking: *(Choukin)*
Alcohol:	Alcohol: *(Alcojol)*
Alergia:	Allergy: *(Alerlii)*
Altura:	Height: *(Jait)*
Amarrar:	Tie: *(Tai)*
Ambulancia:	Ambulance: *(Embiulens)*
Amígdalas:	Tonsils: *(Tansols)*
Andador:	Walker: *(Woker)*
Anemia:	Anemia: *(Animia)*
Antibiótico:	Antibiotic: *(Antibaiatic)*
Antiséptico:	Antiseptic: *(Antiseptic)*
Apendicitis:	Appendicitis: *(Apendisaitis)*
Aplicar:	Apply: *(Aplai)*
Apoyar:	Support: *(Soport)*
Aprete/Pellizque:	Pinch: *(Pinch)*
Ardor:	Burn: *(Bern)*
Articulación:	Joint: *(Lloint)*
Asma:	Asthma: *(Asma)*
Aspirina:	Aspirin: *(Aspirin)*
Ataque:	Attack: *(Atak)*
Auxilio:	Help: *(Jelp)*
Ayuda:	Help: *(Jelp)*
Bastón:	Cane: *(Kein)*
Bendaje:	Bandage: *(Bendech)*

Bolsa de Agua (caliente):	Hot Water Bottle: **(Jat Water Batel)**
Bolsa Fría:	Cold Pack: **(Cold Pak)**
Bolsa de Hielo:	Ice Bag: **(Ais Bag)**
Bulto/Hinchazón/Golpe:	Bump: **(Bamp)**
Busto:	Breast: **(Brest)**
Cachetada:	Slap: **(Slap)**
Caída:	Fall: **(Fol)**
Caspa:	Dandruff: **(Dendruf)**
Cicatríz:	Scar: **(Scar)**
Ciego:	Blind: **(Blaind)**
Clínica:	Clinic: **(Clinic)**
Coágulo de Sangre:	Blood Clot: **(Blad Clat)**
Cobija Eléctrica:	Heating Pad/Electric Blanket: **(Jitin Pad/Eléctric Blanket)**
Compresas:	Compresses: **(Compres)**
Contracción:	Contraction: **(Contracshon)**
Cordón:	Cord: **(Cord)**
Cortada:	Cut: **(Kat)**
Crónico:	Chronic: **(Cronic)**
Cubrir:	Cover: **(Kaver)**
Cuidado:	Care: **(Ker)**
Culebra:	Snake: **(Sneik)**
Curita:	Bandaid: **(Bendei)**
Delicado:	Gentle: **(Llentel)**
Desmayar:	Faint: **(Feint)**
Débil:	Weak: **(Wik)**
Diabetis:	Diabetes: **(Dayabitis)**
Diarrea:	Diarrhea: **(dallaria)**
Dieta:	Diet: **(Daiet)**
Doctor:	Doctor: **(Dactor)**
Dolor de Cabeza:	Headache: **(Jedek)**
Dolor:	Pain/Ache: **(Pein/Eik)**
Droga:	Drug: **(Drag)**
Edad:	Age: **(Eich)**

Embarazada:	Pregnant: *(Pregnant)*
Emergencia:	Emergency: *(Emerllensi)*
Emfermedad:	Illness/Sickness: *(Ilnes/Sicknes)*
Enfermo:	Sick: *(Sick)*
Espinilla/Barrito:	Pimple: *(Pimpel)*
Estéril:	Sterile: *(Sterol)*
Estirar:	To Pull: *(Tu Pul)*
Estreñido:	Constipation: *(Constipeishon)*
Excremento, Heces Fec:	Stool: *(Stul)*
Fiebre:	Fever: *(Fiver)*
Gaza:	Gauze: *(Gos)*
Golpe:	Punch: *(Panch)*
Gotas:	Drops: *(Draps)*
Grande:	Big: *(Big)*
Gripe/Resfriado:	Cold: *(Cold)*
Hemorragia:	Hemorrhage: *(Jemorrech)*
Hemorroide:	Hemorrhoids: *(Jemorroid)*
Herida:	Wound: *(Wund)*
Hinchado:	Swollen: *(Sualen)*
Hongos:	Fungus: *(Fangus)*
Hospital:	Hospital: *(Jaspitol)*
Hueso:	Bone: *(Boun)*
Inconsciente:	Unconscious: *(Ankanshus)*
Infección:	Infection: *(Infecshon)*
Inhale:	Inhale: *(Injeil)*
Injección:	Shot: *(Shat)*
Insolación:	Heat Exhaustion: *(Jit Exaustion)*
Irritación:	Irritation: *(Irriteishon)*
Jarabe:	Syrup: *(Sirop)*
Joven:	Young: *(Llang)*
Lechina/Varicela:	Chicken Pox: *(Chiken Pax)*
Lesión:	Injury: *(Inyuri)*
Levantar:	Lift: *(Lift)*

Limpiar:	Clean: **(Clin)**
Mareado:	Dizzy: **(Dlzi)**
Mareo:	Drowsiness: **(Drausiness)**
Masage:	Massage: **(Masach)**
Medicina:	Medicine: **(Medisin)**
Menopausia:	Menopause: **(Menopos)**
Mental:	Mental: **(Mentol)**
Mesita de Cama:	Bed Tray: **(Bed Trei)**
Mordida:	Bite: **(Bait)**
Mover:	Move: **(Muv)**
Muleta:	Crutch: **(Cratch)**
Náusea:	Nausea: **(Nosha)**
Objeto:	Object: **(Abjject)**
Operación:	Operation/Surgery: **(Opereishon/Serileri)**
Orina:	Urine: **(Llurin)**
Orzuelo:	Sty: **(Stai)**
Oxígeno:	Oxygen: **(Oxillen)**
Paciente:	Patient: **(Peishent)**
Pálido:	Pale: **(Pell)**
Parásitos:	Parasites: **(Peresaites)**
Parálisis:	Palsy **(Polsi)**:
Parto:	Childbirth: **(Chailbers)**
Pastilla:	Pill: **(Pil)**
Pecho:	Chest: **(Chest)**
Peligro:	Danger: **(Denller)**
Pequeña:	Small: **(Smol)**
Peso:	Weight: **(Welt)**
Picada:	Sting: **(Sting)**
Piel:	Skin: **(Skin)**
Policía:	Police: **(Polis)**
Presión:	Pressure: **(Presher)**
Profunda:	Deep: **(Dip)**
Pulso:	Pulse: **(Pols)**
Quemada:	Burn: **(Bern)**

Quiste:	Cyst: *(Sist)*
Rabia:	Rabies: *(Reibis)*
Radiografía:	X-Ray: *(Exrei)*
Raspe:	Scrape: *(Screip)*
Respiración Artificial:	Artificial Respiration: *(Artifishol Respireishon)*
Respirar:	Breath: *(Bris)*
Roto:	Broken: *(Brouken)*
Salpullido/Erupción de la piel:	Rash: *(Rash)* ˘
Salud:	Health: *(Jels)*
Saludable:	Healthy: *(Jelsi)*
Sangrar:	Bleed: *(Blid)*
Sarampión:	Measles: *(Misels)*
Sentir:	Feel: *(Fil)*
Silla de Ruedas:	Wheel Chair: *(Wil Cher)*
Síntomas:	Symptoms: *(Simtoms)*
Sobredosis:	Overdose: *(Overdous)*
Sordo:	Deaf: *(Def)*
Sudor:	Sweat: *(Suet)*
Temperatura:	Temperature: *(Temperachur)*
Termómetro:	Thermometer: *(Termometer)*
Tomar:	Take: *(Teik)*
Torcedura:	Sprain: *(Sprein)*
Tos:	Cough: *(Cof)*
Tragar:	Swallow: *(Sualou)*
Tranquilizar:	Tranquilize: *(Trankulais)*
Transfución:	Transfusion: *(Transfiushon)*
Tratamiento:	Treatment: *(Tritment)*
Tratar:	Treat: *(Trit)*
Tumor:	Tumor: *(Tiumor)*
Vecino:	Neighbor: *(Neibor)*
Venda:	Bandage: *(Bendech)*
Veneno:	Poison: *(Poison)*
Víctima:	Victim: *(Victim)*
'Viejo:	Old: *(Old)*

Virus:	*Virus*: **(Vairus)**
Vitamina:	*Vitamin*: **(Vaitamin)**
Voltée:	*Turn*: **(Tern)**
Vomitar:	*Vomit*: **(Vamit)**
Úlcera:	*Ulcer*: **(Olser)**

Medical Information
(Medikal Informeishon)
Información Médica

Abscess: *(Abses)*	Abseso:
Accident: *(Axident)*	Accidente:
Age: *(Eich)*	Edad:
Alcohol: *(Alcojol)*	Alcohol:
Allergy: *(Alerlli)*	Alergia:
Ambulance: *(Embiulens)*	Ambulancia:
Anemia: *(Animia)*	Anemia:
Antibiotic: *(Antibaiatic)*	Antibiótico:
Antiseptic: *(Antiseptic)*	Antiséptico:
Appendicitis: *(Apendisaitis)*	Apendicitis:
Apply: *(Aplai)*	Aplicar:
Artificial Respiration: *(Artifishol Respireishon)*	
	Respiración Artificial:
Aspirin: *(Aspirin)*	Aspirina:
Asthma: *(Asma)*	Asma:
Attack: *(Atak)*	Ataque:
Bandage: *(Bendech)*	Bendaje:
Bandage: *(Bendech)*	Venda:
Bandaid: *(Bendel)*	Curita:
Bed Tray: *(Bed Trei)*	Mesita de Cama:
Big: *(Big)*	Grande:
Bite: *(Bait)*	Mordida:
Bleed: *(Blid)*	Sangrar:
Blind: *(Blaind)*	Ciego:
Blood Clot: *(Blad Clat)*	Coágulo de Sangre:
Bone: *(Boun)*	Hueso:
Breast: *(Brest)*	Busto:
Breath: *(Bris)*	Respirar:
Broken: *(Brouken)*	Roto:
Bump: *(Bamp)*	Bulto/Hinchazón/Golpe:

Burn: *(Bern)*	Ardor:
Burn: *(Bern)*	Quemada:
Cane: *(Kein)*	Bastón:
Care: *(Ker)*	Cuidado:
Chest: *(Chest)*	Pecho:
Chicken Pox: *(Chiken Pax)*	Lechina/Varicela:
Childbirth: *(Chailbers)*	Parto:
Choking: *(Choukin)*	Ahogado:
Chronic: *(Cronic)*	Crónico:
Clean: *(Clin)*	Limpiar:
Clinic: *(Clinic)*	Clínica:
Cold Pack: *(Cold Pak)*	Bolsa Fría:
Cold: *(Cold)*	Gripe/Resfriado:
Compresses: *(Compres)*	Compresas:
Constipation: *(Constipeishon)*	Estreñido:
Contraction: *(Contracshon)*	Contracción:
Cord: *(Cord)*	Cordón:
Cough: *(Cof)*	Tos:
Cover: *(Kaver)*	Cubrir:
Crutch: *(Cratch)*	Muleta:
Cut: *(Kat)*	Cortada:
Cyst: *(Sist)*	Quiste:
Dandruff: *(Dendruf)*	Caspa:
Danger: *(Denller)*	Peligro:
Deaf: *(Def)*	Sordo:
Deep: *(Dip)*	Profunda:
Diabetes: *(Dayabitis)*	Diabetis:
Diarrhea: *(dallaria)*	Diarrea:
Diet: *(Daiet)*	Dieta:
Dizzy: *(Dizi)*	Mareado:
Doctor: *(Dactor)*	Doctor:
Drops: *(Draps)*	Gotas:
Drowning: *(Draunin)*	Ahogado en Agua:
Drowsiness: *(Drausiness)*	Mareo:
Drug: *(Drag)*	Droga:

Emergency: **(Emerllensi)**	Emergencia:
Faint: **(Feint)**	Desmayar:
Fall: **(Fol)**	Caída:
Feel: **(Fil)**	Sentir:
Fever: **(Fiver)**	Fiebre:
Fungus: **(Fangus)**	Hongos:
Gauze: **(Gos)**	Gaza:
Gentle: **(Llentel)**	Delicado:
Headache: **(Jedek)**	Dolor de Cabeza:
Health: **(Jels)**	Salud:
Healthy: **(Jelsi)**	Saludable:
Heat Exhaustion: **(Jit Exaustion)**	
	Insolación:
Heating Pad/Electric Blanket: **(Jitin Pad/Eléctric Blanket)**	
	Cobija Eléctrica:
Height: **(Jait)**	Altura:
Help: **(Jelp)**	Auxilio:
Help: **(Jelp)**	Ayuda:
Hemorrhage: **(Jemorrech)**	Hemorragia:
Hemorrhoids: **(Jemorroid)**	Hemorroide:
Hospital: **(Jaspitol)**	Hospital:
Hot Water Bottle: **(Jat Water Batel)**	
	Bolsa de Agua(caliente):
Ice Bag: **(Ais Bag)**	Bolsa de Hielo:
Illness/Sickness: **(Ilnes/Sicknes)**	
	Emfermedad:
Infection: **(Infecshon)**	Infección:
Inhale: **(Injeil)**	Inhale:
Injury: **(Inyuri)**	Lesión:
Irritation: **(Irriteishon)**	Irritación:
Joint: **(Lloint)**	Articulación:
Lift: **(Lift)**	Levantar:
Loosen: **(Lusen)**	Afloje:
Lying down: **(Lain daun)**	Acostado:
Massage: **(Masach)**	Masage:

Measles: *(Misels)*	Sarampión:
Medicine: *(Medisin)*	Medicina:
Menopause: *(Menopos)*	Menopausia:
Mental: *(Mentol)*	Mental:
Miscarriage: *(Miskerech)*	Aborto:
Move: *(Muv)*	Mover:
Nausea: *(Nosha)*	Náusea:
Neighbor: *(Neibor)*	Vecino:
Object: *(Abjject)*	Objeto:
Old: *(Old)*	Viejo:
Operation/Surgery: *(Opereishon/Serileri)*	
	Operación:
Overdose: *(Overdous)*	Sobredosis:
Oxygen: *(Oxillen)*	Oxígeno:
Pain/Ache: *(Pein/Eik)*	Dolor:
Pale: *(Peil)*	Pálido:
Palsy:	Parálisis:
Parasites: *(Peresaites)*	Parásitos:
Patient: *(Peishent)*	Paciente:
Pill: *(Pil)*	Pastilla:
Pimple: *(Pimpel)*	Espinilla/Barrito:
Pinch: *(Pinch)*	Aprete/Pellizque:
Poison: *(Poison)*	Veneno:
Police: *(Polis)*	Policía:
Pregnant: *(Pregnant)*	Embarazada:
Pressure: *(Presher)*	Presión:
Pulse: *(Pols)*	Pulso:
Punch: *(Panch)*	Golpe:
Rabies: *(Reibis)*	Rabia:
Rash: *(Rash)*	Salpullido/Erupción de la piel:
Scar: *(Scar)*	Cicatríz:
Scrape: *(Screip)*	Raspe:
Shot: *(Shat)*	Injección:
Sick: *(Sick)*	Enfermo:
Skin: *(Skin)*	Piel:

Slap: *(Slap)*	Cachetada:
Small: *(Smol)*	Pequeña:
Snake: *(Sneik)*	Culebra:
Sprain: *(Sprein)*	Torcedura:
Sterile: *(Sterol)*	Estéril:
Sting: *(Sting)*	Picada:
Stool: *(Stul)*	Excremento, Heces Fec:
Sty: *(Stai)*	Orzuelo:
Support: *(Soport)*	Apoyar:
Swallow: *(Sualou)*	Tragar:
Sweat: *(Suet)*	Sudor:
Swollen: *(Sualen)*	Hinchado:
Symptoms: *(Simtoms)*	Síntomas:
Syrup: *(Sirop)*	Jarabe:
Take: *(Teik)*	Tomar:
Temperature: *(Temperachur)*	Temperatura:
Thermometer: *(Termometer)*	Termómetro:
Tie: *(Tai)*	Amarrar:
To Pull: *(Tu Pul)*	Estirar:
Tonsils: *(Tansols)*	Amígdalas:
Tranquilize: *(Trankulais)*	Tranquilizar:
Transfusion: *(Transfiushon)*	Transfución:
Treat: *(Trit)*	Tratar:
Treatment: *(Tritment)*	Tratamiento:
Tumor: *(Tiumor)*	Tumor:
Turn: *(Tern)*	Voltée:
Ulcer: *(Olser)*	Úlcera:
Unconscious: *(Ankanshus)*	Inconsciente:
Urine: *(Llurin)*	Orina:
Victim: *(Victim)*	Víctima:
Virus: *(Vairus)*	Virus:
Vitamin: *(Vaitamin)*	Vitamina:
Vomit: *(Vamit)*	Vomitar:
Walker: *(Woker)*	Andador:
Weak: *(Wik)*	Débil:

Weight: **(Welt)**	Peso:
Wheel Chair: **(Wil Cher)**	Silla de Ruedas:
Wound: **(Wund)**	Herida:
X-Ray: **(Exrei)**	Radiografía:
Young: **(Llang)**	Joven:

Maneras de Cocinar
Ways of Cooking
(Kuking Weis)

Adobar/Sazonar:	Season: *(Sison)*
Agitar:	Shake: *(Sheik)*
Agregar/Añadir:	Add: *(Ad)*
Amasar:	Knead: *(Knid)*
Asar:	Grill: *(Gril)*
Bañar/Inmercir:	Dip: *(Dip)*
Baño María:	Double Boil: *(Dabel Boil)*
Batir:	Beat: *(Bit)*
Brasar:	Broil: *(Broil)*
Calentar:	Heat/Warm Up: *(Hit/Wuorm Ap)*
Cocinar al Fuego Lento:	Simmer: *(Simer)*
Cocine:	Cook: *(Kuk)*
Colar:	Strain: *(Strein)*
Conservar:	Keep: *(Kip)*
Cortar:	Cut: *(Kat)*
Cubrir:	Cover: *(Kaver)*
Decorar:	Decorate: *(Decoreit)*
Derretir:	Melt: *(Melt)*
Descongelar:	Defrost: *(Difrost)*
Disolver:	Dissolve: *(Disolv)*
Dorar:	Brown: *(Braun)*
Enfriar:	Cool: *(Kul)*
Engrase:	Grease: *(Gris)*
Freir:	Fry: *(Frai)*
Guisar:	Stew: *(Stu)*
Hervir:	Boil: *(Boil)*
Hornear/Cocer:	Bake: *(Beik)*
Lavar:	Wash: *(Wash)*
Limpiar:	Clean: *(Klin)*
Machacar:	Mash: *(Mash)*

Marinar:	Marinate: *(Merineit)*
Mezclar:	Mix: *(Mix)*
Moler:	Grind: *(Graind)*
Pelar:	Peel: *(Pil)*
Picar:	Chop: *(Chap)*
Polvorear:	Dusting: *(Dastin)*
Preparar:	Prepare: *(Priper)*
Quemar:	Burn: *(Bern)*
Rallar:	Grate: *(Greit)*
Rebanar:	Slice: *(Slais)*
Rellenar:	Stuffed: *(Staf)*
Remojar:	Soak: *(Souk)*
Revolver:	Stir: *(Ster)*
Secar:	Dry: *(Drai)*
Servir:	Serve: *(Serv)*
Sofrito/Sofreir:	Sauté: *(Saute)*
Tostar:	Toast: *(Toust)*
Untar:	Spread: *(Spred)*
Vertir:	Pour: *(Pur)*

Ways of Cooking
(Kuking Weis)
Maneras de Cocinar

Add: *(Ad)*	Agregar/Añadir:
Bake: *(Beik)*	Hornear/Cocer:
Beat: *(Bit)*	Batir:
Boil: *(Boil)*	Hervir:
Broil: *(Broil)*	Brasar:
Brown: *(Braun)*	Dorar:
Burn: *(Bern)*	Quemar:
Chop: *(Chap)*	Picar:
Clean: *(Klin)*	Limpiar:
Cook: *(Kuk)*	Cocine:
Cool: *(Kul)*	Enfriar:
Cover: *(Kaver)*	Cubrir:
Cut: *(Kat)*	Cortar:
Decorate: *(Decoreit)*	Decorar:
Defrost: *(Difrost)*	Descongelar:
Dip: *(Dip)*	Bañar/Inmercir:
Dissolve: *(Disolv)*	Disolver:
Double Boil: *(Dabel Boil)*	Baño María:
Dry: *(Drai)*	Secar:
Dusting: *(Dastin)*	Polvorear:
Fry: *(Frai)*	Freir:
Grate: *(Greit)*	Rallar:
Grease: *(Gris)*	Engrase:
Grill: *(Gril)*	Asar:
Grind: *(Graind)*	Moler:
Heat/Warm Up: *(Hit/Wuorm Ap)*	Calentar:
Keep: *(Kip)*	Conservar:
Knead: *(Knid)*	Amasar:
Marinate: *(Merineit)*	Marinar:
Mash: *(Mash)*	Machacar:

Melt: *(Melt)*	Derretir:
Mix: *(Mix)*	Mezclar:
Peel: *(Pil)*	Pelar:
Pour: *(Pur)*	Vertir:
Prepare: *(Priper)*	Preparar:
Sauté: *(Saute)*	Sofrito/Sofreir:
Season: *(Sison)*	Adobar/Sazonar:
Serve: *(Serv)*	Servir:
Shake: *(Sheik)*	Agitar:
Simmer: *(Simer)*	Cocinar al Fuego Lento:
Slice: *(Slais)*	Rebanar:
Soak: *(Souk)*	Remojar:
Spread: *(Spred)*	Untar:
Stew: *(Stu)*	Guisar:
Stir: *(Ster)*	Revolver:
Strain: *(Strein)*	Colar:
Stuffed: *(Staf)*	Rellenar:
Toast: *(Toust)*	Tostar:
Wash: *(Wash)*	Lavar:

Recetas:
Recipes:
(Resepis):

Recetas:
Recipes:
(Resepis):

Recetas:
Recipes:
(Resepis):

Recetas:
Recipes:
(Resepis):

Recetas:
Recipes:
(Resepis):

Recetas:
Recipes:
(Resepis):

Lugares
Places
(Pleices)

Aeropuerto:	Airport: *(Erport)*
Agencia de Viajes:	Travel Agency: *(Travel Eillensi)*
Apartamento:	Apartment: *(Apartment)*
Avión:	Airplane: *(Erplein)*
Bailar:	Dance: *(Dens)*
Banco:	Bank: *(Benk)*
Barco:	Ship/Boat: *(Ship/Bout)*
Biblioteca:	Library: *(Laibrari)*
Calle:	Street: *(Strit)*
Casa:	House: *(Jaus)*
Centro Comercial:	Mall: *(Mol)*
Centro de la Ciudad:	Downtown: *(Dauntaun)*
Cine:	Movie Theater: *(Muvi Tiater)*
Ciudad:	City: *(Siti)*
Colegio/Escuela:	School: *(Skul)*
Compras:	Shopping: *(Shapin)*
Correo (Estación):	Post Office: *(Poust Ofis)*
Edificio:	Building: *(Bilding)*
Estación:	Station: *(Estaishon)*
Farmacia:	Pharmacy: *(Farmasi)*
Ferretería:	Hardware Store: *(Jardwer Stor)*
Fiesta:	Party: *(Parti)*
Frutería:	Fruit Market: *(Frut Market)*
Gasolinera:	Gas Station: *(Gas Esteishon)*
Gimnasio:	Gym: *(Llim)*
Hospital:	Hospital: *(Jaspitol)*
Iglesia:	Church: *(Cherch)*
Juego:	Game: *(Geim)*
Jugar:	Play: *(Plei)*
Juguetería:	Toy Store: *(Toi Stor)*

Librería:	Book Store: **(Buk Stor)**
Montaña:	Mountain: **(Maunten)**
Mueblería:	Furniture Store: **(Furnichur Stor)**
Museo:	Museum: **(Miusium)**
Oficina:	Office: **(Ofis)**
País:	Country: **(Kauntri)**
Parque:	Park: **(Park)**
Pastelería:	Bakery: **(Beikeri)**
Peluquería:	Beauty Shop: **(Biuti Shap)**
Playa:	Beach: **(Bich)**
Pueblo:	Town: **(Taun)**
Puerto:	Port: **(Port)**
Restaurante:	Restaurant: **(Restaurant)**
Río:	River: **(River)**
Supermercado:	Grocery Store/Supermarket: **(Groceri-Stor/Supermarket)**
Teatro:	Theater: **(Tiater)**
Teléfono Público:	Pay Phone: **(Pei Fon)**
Tienda:	Store: **(Stor)**
Tintorería/Lavandería:	Cleaners: **(Kliners)**
Trabajo:	Work: **(Wourk)**
Universidad:	College/University: **(Colech/Yuniversiti)**
Zoológico:	Zoo: **(Zu)**

Places
(Pleices)
Lugares

Airplane: **(Erplein)**   Avión:

Airport: **(Erport)**   Aeropuerto:

Apartment: **(Apartment)**   Apartamento:

Bakery: **(Beikeri)**   Pastelería:

Bank: **(Benk)**   Banco:

Beach: **(Bich)**   Playa:

Beauty Shop: **(Biuti Shap)**   Peluquería:

Book Store: **(Buk Stor)**   Librería:

Building: **(Bilding)**   Edificio:

Church: **(Cherch)**   Iglesia:

City: **(Siti)**   Ciudad:

Cleaners: **(Kliners)**   Tintorería/Lavandería:

College/University: **(Colech/Yuniversiti)**

     Universidad:

Country: **(Kauntri)**   País:

Dance: **(Dens)**   Bailar:

Downtown: **(Dauntaun)**   Centro de la Ciudad:

Fruit Market: **(Frut Market)**   Frutería:

Furniture Store: **(Furnichur Stor)**

     Mueblería:

Game: **(Geim)**   Juego:

Gas Station: **(Gas Esteishon)**   Gasolinera:

Grocery Store/Supermarket: **(Groceri-Stor/Supermarket)**

     Supermercado:

Gym: **(Llim)**   Gimnasio:

Hardware Store: **(Jardwer Stor)**   Ferretería:

Hospital: **(Jaspitol)**   Hospital:

House: **(Jaus)**   Casa:

Library: **(Laibrari)**   Biblioteca:

Mall: **(Mol)**   Centro Comercial:

Mountain: *(Maunten)*	Montaña:
Movie Theater: *(Muvi Tiater)*	Cine:
Museum: *(Miusium)*	Museo:
Office: *(Ofis)*	Oficina:
Park: *(Park)*	Parque:
Party: *(Parti)*	Fiesta:
Pay Phone: *(Pei Fon)*	Teléfono Público:
Pharmacy: *(Farmasi)*	Farmacia:
Play: *(Plei)*	Jugar:
Port: *(Port)*	Puerto:
Post Office: *(Poust Ofis)*	Correo (Estación):
Restaurant: *(Restaurant)*	Restaurante:
River: *(River)*	Río:
School: *(Skul)*	Colegio/Escuela:
Ship/Boat: *(Ship/Bout)*	Barco:
Shopping: *(Shapin)*	Compras:
Station: *(Estaishon)*	Estación:
Store: *(Stor)*	Tienda:
Street: *(Strit)*	Calle:
Theater: *(Tiater)*	Teatro:
Town: *(Taun)*	Pueblo:
Toy Store: *(Toi Stor)*	Juguetería:
Travel Agency: *(Travel EiIensi)*	Agencia de Viajes:
Work: *(Wourk)*	Trabajo:
Zoo: *(Zu)*	Zoológico:

Personas / Roles / Trabajos
People / Roles / Jobs
(Pipol / Rouls / Yabs)

Abogado:	Lawyer: **(Loyer)**
Abuela:	Grandmother: **(Grenmader)**
Abuelo:	Grandfather: **(Grenfader)**
Agente de Viajes:	Travel Agent: **(Travel Eigent)**
Albañil:	Mason: **(Meison)**
Amigo(a):	Friend: **(Frend)**
Arquitecto:	Architect: **(Arquitect)**
Artista:	Artist: **(Artist)**
Autobusero:	Bus Driver: **(Bas Draiver)**
Barbero:	Barber: **(Barber)**
Bombero:	Fireman: **(Faiermen)**
Cajero:	Cashier: **(Cashir)**
Camionero:	Truck Driver: **(Trak Draiver)**
Cantante:	Singer: **(Singer)**
Carnicero:	Butcher: **(Bucher)**
Carpintero:	Carpenter: **(Carpinter)**
Cartero:	Mailman: **(Meilmen)**
Chofer/Conductor:	Driver/Chauffeur: **(Draiver)**
Comerciante:	Business man: **(Bisnes men)**
Compañero(a) de clase:	Classmate: **(Clasmeit)**
Comprometido:	Fiancé: **(Fianse)**
Costurera:	Seamstress: **(Simstres)**
Criada:	Housekeeper: **(Jauskiper)**
Cura:	Monk: **(Mank)**
Decoradora:	Decorator: **(Decoreitor)**
Dentista:	Dentist: **(Dentist)**
Director:	Director: **(Director)**
Doctor:	Doctor: **(Dactor)**
Dueño:	Owner: **(Ouner)**
Electricista:	Electrician: **(Electrishan)**

Enemigo:	Enemy: *(Enemi)*
Enfermera(o):	Nurse: *(Ners)*
Escritor:	Writer: *(Wralter)*
Esposa:	Wife: *(Waif)*
Esposo:	Husband: *(Jasband)*
Estudiante:	Student: *(Student)*
Floristero:	Florist: *(Florist)*
Gerente:	Manager: *(Manayer)*
Hermana:	Sister: *(Sister)*
Hermano:	Brother: *(Brader)*
Hija:	Daughter: *(Douter)*
Hijo:	Son: *(San)*
Hombre:	Man: *(Men)*
Ingeniero:	Engineer: *(Inllenir)*
Jardinero:	Yardman: *(Yardmen)*
Jefe:	Chief: *(Chif)*
Madre:	Mother: *(Mader)*
Manicurista:	Manicurist: *(Manikurist)*
Mayordomo:	Butler: *(Batler)*
Mecánico:	Mechanic: *(Mecanic)*
Mesonero/Mesero:	Waiter: *(Welter)*
Monja:	Nun: *(Nan)*
Mujer:	Woman: *(Wumen)*
Músico:	Musician: *(Miusishan)*
Nieta:	Granddaughter: *(Grendoter)*
Nieto:	Grandson: *(Grenson)*
Niña/Hembra:	Girl: *(Gerl)*
Niño/Varón:	Boy: *(Boi)*
Niños:	Children: *(Children)*
Novia:	Girlfriend: *(Gerlfrend)*
Novio:	Boyfriend: *(Boifrend)*
Nuera:	Daughter-in-Law: *(Doter-in-Lo)*
Obrero:	Worker (Labor): *(Worker)*
Operador(a):	Operator: *(Opereitor)*
Padre:	Father: *(Fader)*

Panadera:	Baker: *(Beiker)*
Pastor:	Priest: *(Prist)*
Peluquero(a):	Hairdresser: *(Jerdreser)*
Piloto:	Pilot: *(Pallot)*
Pintor:	Painter: *(Peintor)*
Plomero:	Plumber: *(Plamer)*
Policía:	Policeman: *(Polismen)*
Primo:	Cousin: *(Kasen)*
Profesora/Maestra:	Teacher: *(Ticher)*
Secretaria:	Secretary: *(Sekreteri)*
Señor:	Mr.: *(Mister)*
Señora:	Mrs.: *(Mises)*
Señorita:	Miss: *(Mis)*
Suegra:	Mother-in-Law: *(Mader-in-Lo)*
Suegro:	Father-in-Law: *(Fader-in-Lo)*
Taxista:	Taxi Driver: *(Taxi Draiver)*
Tía:	Aunt: *(Ent)*
Tío:	Uncle: *(Ankel)*
Trabajador:	Worker: *(Worker)*
Vecino:	Neighbor: *(Neibor)*
Vendedora:	Salesperson: *(Seilsperson)*
Yerno:	Son-in-Law: *(San-in-Lo)*
Zapatero:	Shoe Repair Man: *(Shu-Ripermen)*

People / Roles / Jobs
(Pipol / Rouls / Yabs)
Personas / Roles / Trabajos

Architect: *(Arquitect)*   Arquitecto:
Artist: *(Artist)*   Artista:
Aunt: *(Ent)*   Tía:
Baker: *(Beiker)*   Panadera:
Barber: *(Barber)*   Barbero:
Boy: *(Boi)*   Niño/Varón:
Boyfriend: *(Boifrend)*   Novio:
Brother: *(Brader)*   Hermano:
Bus Driver: *(Bas Draiver)*   Autobusero:
Business man: *(Bisnes men)*   Comerciante:
Butcher: *(Bucher)*   Carnicero:
Butler: *(Batler)*   Mayordomo:
Carpenter: *(Carpinter)*   Carpintero:
Cashier: *(Cashir)*   Cajero:
Chief: *(Chif)*   Jefe:
Children: *(Children)*   Niños:
Classmate: *(Clasmeit)*   Compañero(a) de clase:
Cousin: *(Kasen)*   Primo:
Daughter-in-Law: *(Doter-in-Lo)*   Nuera:
Daughter: *(Douter)*   Hija:
Decorator: *(Decoreitor)*   Decoradora:
Dentist: *(Dentist)*   Dentista:
Director: *(Director)*   Director:
Doctor: *(Dactor)*   Doctor:
Driver/Chauffeur: *(Draiver)*   Chofer/Conductor:
Electrician: *(Electrishan)*   Electricista:
Enemy: *(Enemi)*   Enemigo:
Engineer: *(Inilenir)*   Ingeniero:
Father-in-Law: *(Fader-in-Lo)*   Suegro:
Father: *(Fader)*   Padre:

Fiancé: *(Fianse)*	Comprometido:
Fireman: *(Faiermen)*	Bombero:
Florist: *(Florist)*	Floristero:
Friend: *(Frend)*	Amigo(a):
Girl: *(Gerl)*	Niña/Hembra:
Girlfriend: *(Gerlfrend)*	Novia:
Granddaughter: *(Grendoter)*	Nieta:
Grandfather: *(Grenfader)*	Abuelo:
Grandmother: *(Grenmader)*	Abuela:
Grandson: *(Grenson)*	Nieto:
Hairdresser: *(Jerdreser)*	Peluquero(a):
Housekeeper: *(Jauskiper)*	Criada:
Husband: *(Jasband)*	Esposo:
Lawyer: *(Loyer)*	Abogado:
Mailman: *(Meilmen)*	Cartero:
Man: *(Men)*	Hombre:
Manager: *(Manayer)*	Gerente:
Manicurist: *(Manikurist)*	Manicurista:
Mason: *(Meison)*	Albañil:
Mechanic: *(Mecanic)*	Mecánico:
Miss: *(Mis)*	Señorita:
Monk: *(Mank)*	Cura:
Mother-in-Law: *(Mader-in-Lo)*	Suegra:
Mother: *(Mader)*	Madre:
Mr.: *(Mister)*	Señor:
Mrs.: *(Mises)*	Señora:
Musician: *(Miusishan)*	Músico:
Neighbor: *(Neibor)*	Vecino:
Nun: *(Nan)*	Monja:
Nurse: *(Ners)*	Enfermera(o):
Operator: *(Opereitor)*	Operador(a):
Owner: *(Ouner)*	Dueño:
Painter: *(Peintor)*	Pintor:
Pilot: *(Pailot)*	Piloto:
Plumber: *(Plamer)*	Plomero:

Policeman: *(Polismen)*	Policía:
Priest: *(Prist)*	Pastor:
Salesperson: *(Seilsperson)*	Vendedora:
Seamstress: *(Simstres)*	Costurera:
Secretary: *(Sekreteri)*	Secretaria:
Shoe Repair Man: *(Shu- Ripermen)*	
	Zapatero:
Singer: *(Singer)*	Cantante:
Sister: *(Sister)*	Hermana:
Son-in-Law: *(San-in-Lo)*	Yerno:
Son: *(San)*	Hijo:
Student: *(Student)*	Estudiante:
Taxi Driver: *(Taxi Draiver)*	Taxista:
Teacher: *(Ticher)*	Profesora/Maestra:
Travel Agent: *(Travel Eigent)*	Agente de Viajes:
Truck Driver: *(Trak Draiver)*	Camionero:
Uncle: *(Ankel)*	Tío:
Waiter: *(Weiter)*	Mesonero/Mesero:
Wife: *(Walf)*	Esposa:
Woman: *(Wumen)*	Mujer:
Worker (Labor): *(Worker)*	Obrero:
Worker: *(Worker)*	Trabajador:
Writer: *(Wraiter)*	Escritor:
Yardman: *(Yardmen)*	Jardinero:

Palabras Extras
Extra Words
(Extra Wourds)

Aduana:	Custom House: **(Kastom Jaus)**
Agrio/Acido:	Sour: **(Sauer)**
Ahora Mismo:	Right Now: **(Rait Nau)**
Aire:	Air: **(Er)**
Alguien:	Someone: **(Som-uan)**
Algún:	Any: **(Eni)**
Alguna Vez:	Ever: **(Ever)**
Algunas Veces:	Sometimes: **(Somtaims)**
Ambos:	Both: **(Bous)**
Arruinado:	Broke: **(Brouk)**
Asegurar:	Insure: **(Inshur)**
Asiento:	Seat: **(Sit)**
Aún:	Even: **(Iven)**
Ausente:	Absent: **(Absent)**
Bajar:	Get Off: **(Get Of)**
Banco:	Bank: **(Benk)**
Buscar:	Look For: **(Luk For)**
Cada:	Each: **(Ich)**
Calendario:	Calendar: **(Calender)**
Cambio:	Change: **(Cheinch)**
Caminar:	Walk: **(Wok)**
Cana:	Gray Hair: **(Grei Jer)**
Carbón:	Coals: **(Coils)**
Carta:	Letter: **(Leter)**
Cartelera:	Bulletin Board: **(Boliten Bord)**
Ceniza:	Ash: **(Ash)**
Cinturón de Seguridad:	Seat Belt: **(Sit Belt)**
Clase/Variedad:	Kind: **(Kaind)**
Coleccionar:	Collect: **(Colect)**
Con Frecuencia:	Often: **(Often)**

Con:	With: **(Wis)**
Conocer:	Meet: **(Mit)**
Cómodo:	Comfortable: **(Comfterbol)**
Costumbre:	Costum: **(Kastum)**
Cuánto Tiempo:	How Long: **(Jau Long)**
Cuentas:	Bills: **(Bils)**
Cuidadosamente:	Carefully: **(Kerfuli)**
Cuidadoso:	Careful: **(Kerful)**
Debajo:	Under: **(Ander)**
Deber:	Must: **(Mast)**
Decidir:	Decide: **(Disaid)**
Decir:	Say: **(Sei)**
Delante:	Ahead: **(Ajed)**
Derecha:	Right: **(Rait)**
Derramar:	Sprinkle: **(Sprinkel)**
Descontar:	Discount: **(Discaunt)**
Desear:	Wish: **(Wish)**
Deseo:	(A) Wish: **(El Wish)**
Detrás:	Behind: **(Bijaind)**
Diccionario:	Dictionary: **(Dicshoneri)**
Dieta:	Diet: **(Daiet)**
Difícil:	Difficult: **(Dificolt)**
Dios:	God: **(Gad)**
Dólar:	Dollar: **(Dolar)**
Dulce:	Sweet: **(Suit)**
Efectivo:	Cash: **(Cash)**
En:	At: **(At)**
Encima:	On: **(On)**
Entrada:	Gate: **(Geit)**
Entregar:	Deliver: **(Deliver)**
Enviar/Mandar:	Send: **(Send)**
Equivocado:	Wrong: **(Wrong)**
Esconder:	Hide: **(Jid)**
Eso:	That: **(Dat)**
Esquina:	Corner: **(Korner)**

Estampilla:	Stamp: *(Stemp)*
Estrella:	Star: *(Star)*
Familia:	Family: *(Femili)*
Fácil:	Easy: *(Isi)*
Fila:	Line: *(Lain)*
Fresco:	Cool: *(Kul)*
Fuera:	Away: *(Ewei)*
Futuro:	Future: *(Fiucher)*
Ganar:	Win: *(Wuin)*
Gracioso:	Funny: *(Fani)*
Hacer:	Do: *(Du)*
Hay:	There Is: *(Der Is)*
Hermoso:	Beautiful: *(Biutiful)*
Idioma/Lenguaje:	Language: *(Lenguech)*
Insectos:	Insects: *(Insects)*
Invierno:	Winter: *(Winter)*
Izquierda:	Left: *(Left)*
Juntos:	Together: *(Tugeder)*
Jurar:	Swear: *(Suer)*
Ladrillo:	Brick: *(Brik)*
Lápiz:	Pencil: *(Pencil)*
Levantar:	Get Up: *(Get Ap)*
Listo:	Ready: *(Redi)*
Llegar:	Arrive: *(Araiv)*
Llenar:	Fill: *(Fil)*
Lluvia:	Rain: *(Rein)*
Luna:	Moon: *(Mun)*
Maleta/Petaca:	Suitcase: *(Sutkeis)*
Maravilloso:	Wonderful *(Wonderful)*
Mármol:	Marble: *(Marbol)*
Máquina de Coser:	Sewing Machine: *(Soin Mashin)*
Máquina de Escribir:	Typewriter: *(Taip Raiter)*
Más Tarde:	Later: *(Leiter)*
Medio/Mitad:	Half: *(Jaf)*
Mejor:	Better: *(Beter)*

Meser:	Swing: *(Suing)*
Mirar:	Look: *(Luk)*
Motor:	Motor: *(Moutor)*
Muestra:	Sample: *(Sempel)*
Muy:	Very: *(Veri)*
Nieve:	Snow: *(Snou)*
Noche:	Evening: *(Ivnin)*
Nuestro:	Our: *(Auer)*
Oir:	Hear: *(Jir)*
Otoño:	Fall/Autumn: *(Fol/Otom)*
Pagos:	Payments: *(Pelments)*
Paquete:	Package: *(Pakech)*
Par:	Pair: *(Per)*
Pasado:	Pass: *(Pas)*
Pasaporte:	Passport: *(Pasport)*
Patinar:	Skate: *(Skeit)*
Patio:	Backyard: *(Bakyard)*
Pedazo:	Piece: *(Pis)*
Pegajoso:	Sticky: *(Stiki)*
Pelota:	Ball: *(Bol)*
Pensar:	Think: *(Sink)*
Perder:	Loose: *(Lus)*
Pero:	But: *(Bat)*
Pesado:	Heavy: *(Jevi)*
Pito:	Whistle: *(Wisol)*
Planear:	Plan: *(Plen)*
Pluma:	Pen: *(Pen)*
Por Fín:	Finally: *(Faineli)*
Por:	By: *(Bai)*
Porque:	Because: *(Bicos)*
Postre:	Dessert: *(Desert)*
Practicar:	Practice: *(Practis)*
Precio:	Price: *(Prais)*
Pregunta:	Question: *(Kuestion)*
Preparar:	Prepare: *(Pripér)*

Primavera:	Spring: *(Spring)*
Puedo:	May: *(Mei)*
Queja:	Complain: *(Complain)*
Quitarse:	Take Off: *(Teik Of)*
Raspar:	Scour/Scrape: *(Scor/Skreip)*
Rato:	While: *(Wail)*
Receta Médica:	Prescription: *(Prescripshon)*
Religión:	Religion: *(Relillon)*
Reporte:	Report: *(Riport)*
Rezar/Orar:	Pray: *(Prei)*
Robar:	Steal: *(Stil)*
Rueda:	Tire: *(Taier)*
Salvaje:	Wild: *(Waild)*
Semáforo:	Traffic Light: *(Trafic Lait)*
Sol:	Sun: *(San)*
Soplar:	Blow: *(Blou)*
Subir:	Get On: *(Get On)*
Sujeta/Agarra:	Hold: *(Jold)*
Tal:	Such: *(Sach)*
También:	Also: *(Olso)*
Tampoco:	Either: *(Ider)*
Tener Sueño:	Sleepy: *(Slipi)*
Terminar:	End: *(End)*
Tierra:	Earth: *(Ers)*
Traer:	Bring: *(Bring)*
Un:	A: *(Ei)*
Vacación:	Vacation: *(Vakeishon)*
Venir:	Come: *(Kam)*
Verano:	Summer: *(Samer)*
Viajar:	Travel: *(Travel)*
Viaje:	Trip: *(Trip)*
Vidrio:	Glass: *(Glass)*
Volver:	Return: *(Riturn)*

Extra Words
(Extra Wourds)
Palabras Extras

A: *(Ei)*	Un:
Absent: *(Absent)*	Ausente:
Ahead: *(Ajed)*	Delante:
Air: *(Er)*	Aire:
Also: *(Olso)*	También:
Any: *(Eni)*	Algún:
Arrive: *(Araiv)*	Llegar:
Ash: *(Ash)*	Ceniza:
At: *(At)*	En:
Away: *(Ewei)*	Fuera:
Backyard: *(Bakyard)*	Patio:
Ball: *(Bol)*	Pelota:
Bank: *(Benk)*	Banco:
Beautiful: *(Biutiful)*	Hermoso:
Because: *(Bicos)*	Porque:
Behind: *(Bijaind)*	Detrás:
Better: *(Beter)*	Mejor:
Bills: *(Bils)*	Cuentas:
Blow: *(Blou)*	Soplar:
Both: *(Bous)*	Ambos:
Brick: *(Bric)*	Ladrillo:
Bring: *(Bring)*	Traer:
Broke: *(Brouk)*	Arruinado:
Bulletin Board: *(Boliten Bord)*	Cartelera:
But: *(Bat)*	Pero:
By: *(Bai)*	Por:
Calendar: *(Calender)*	Calendario:
Careful: *(Kerful)*	Cuidadoso:
Carefully: *(Kerfuli)*	Cuidadosamente:
Cash: *(Cash)*	Efectivo:

Change: *(Cheinch)*	Cambio:
Coals: *(Coils)*	Carbón:
Collect: *(Colect)*	Coleccionar:
Come: *(Kam)*	Venir:
Comfortable: *(Comfterbol)*	Cómodo:
Complain: *(Complain)*	Queja:
Cool: *(Kul)*	Fresco:
Corner: *(Korner)*	Esquina:
Custom: *(Kastom)*	Costumbre:
Custom House: *(Kastom Jaus)*	Aduana:
Decide: *(Disaid)*	Decidir:
Deliver: *(Deliver)*	Entregar:
Dessert: *(Desert)*	Postre:
Dictionary: *(Dicshoneri)*	Diccionario:
Diet: *(Daiet)*	Dieta:
Difficult: *(Dificolt)*	Difícil:
Discount: *(Discaunt)*	Descontar:
Do: *(Du)*	Hacer:
Dollar: *(Dolar)*	Dólar:
Each: *(Ich)*	Cada:
Earth: *(Ers)*	Tierra:
Easy: *(Isi)*	Fácil:
Either: *(Ider)*	Tampoco:
End: *(End)*	Terminar:
Even: *(Iven)*	Aún:
Evening: *(Ivnin)*	Noche:
Ever: *(Ever)*	Alguna Vez:
Fall/Autumn: *(Fol/Otom)*	Otoño:
Family: *(Femili)*	Familia:
Fill: *(Fil)*	Llenar:
Finally: *(Fainell)*	Por Fín:
Funny: *(Fani)*	Gracioso:
Future: *(Fiucher)*	Futuro:
Gate: *(Geit)*	Entrada:
Get Off: *(Get Of)*	Bajar:

Get On: *(Get On)*	Subir:
Get Up: *(Get Ap)*	Levantar:
Glass: *(Glas)*	Vidrio:
God: *(Gad)*	Dios:
Gray Hair: *(Grei Jer)*	Cana:
Half: *(Jaf)*	Medio/Mitad:
Hear: *(Jir)*	Oir:
Heavy: *(Jevi)*	Pesado:
Hide: *(Jid)*	Esconder:
Hold: *(Jold)*	Sujeta/Agarra:
How Long: *(Jau Long)*	Cuánto Tiempo:
Insects: *(Insects)*	Insectos:
Insure: *(Inshur)*	Asegurar:
Kind: *(Kaind)*	Clase/Variedad:
Language: *(Lenguech)*	Idioma/Lenguaje:
Later: *(Leiter)*	Más Tarde:
Left: *(Left)*	Izquierda:
Letter: *(Leter)*	Carta:
Line: *(Lain)*	Fila:
Look For: *(Luk For)*	Buscar:
Look: *(Luk)*	Mirar:
Loose: *(Lus)*	Perder:
Marble: *(Marbol)*	Mármol:
May: *(Mei)*	Puedo:
Meet: *(Mit)*	Conocer:
Moon: *(Mun)*	Luna:
Motor: *(Moutor)*	Motor:
Must: *(Mast)*	Deber:
Often: *(Often)*	Con Frecuencia:
On: *(On)*	Encima:
Our: *(Auer)*	Nuestro:
Package: *(Pakech)*	Paquete:
Pair: *(Per)*	Par:
Pass: *(Pas)*	Pasado:
Passport: *(Pasport)*	Pasaporte:

Payments: *(Peiments)*	Pagos:
Pen: *(Pen)*	Pluma:
Pencil: *(Pencil)*	Lápiz:
Piece: *(Pis)*	Pedazo:
Plan: *(Plen)*	Planear:
Practice: *(Practis)*	Practicar:
Pray: *(Prei)*	Rezar/Orar:
Prepare: *(Pripér)*	Preparar:
Prescription: *(Prescripshon)*	Receta Médica:
Price: *(Prais)*	Precio:
Question: *(Kuestion)*	Pregunta:
Rain: *(Rein)*	Lluvia:
Ready: *(Redi)*	Listo:
Religion: *(Relilion)*	Religión:
Report: *(Riport)*	Reporte:
Return: *(Riturn)*	Volver:
Right Now: *(Rait Nau)*	Ahora Mismo:
Right: *(Rait)*	Derecha:
Sample: *(Sempel)*	Muestra:
Say: *(Sei)*	Decir:
Scour/Scrape: *(Scor/Skreip)*	Raspar:
Seat Belt: *(Sit Belt)*	Cinturón de Seguridad:
Seat: *(Sit)*	Asiento:
Send: *(Send)*	Enviar/Mandar:
Sewing Machine: *(Soin Mashin)*	Máquina de Coser:
Skate: *(Skeit)*	Patinar:
Sleepy: *(Slipi)*	Tener Sueño:
Snow: *(Snou)*	Nieve:
Someone: *(Som-uan)*	Alguien:
Sometimes: *(Somtaims)*	Algunas Veces:
Sour: *(Sauer)*	Agrio/Acido:
Spring: *(Spring)*	Primavera:
Sprinkle: *(Sprinkel)*	Derramar:
Stamp: *(Stemp)*	Estampilla:
Star: *(Star)*	Estrella:

Steal: *(Stil)*	Robar:
Sticky: *(Stiki)*	Pegajoso:
Such: *(Sach)*	Tal:
Suitcase: *(Sutkeis)*	Maleta/Petaca:
Summer: *(Samer)*	Verano:
Sun: *(San)*	Sol:
Swear: *(Suer)*	Jurar:
Sweet: *(Suit)*	Dulce:
Swing: *(Suing)*	Meser:
Take Off: *(Teik Of)*	Quitarse:
That: *(Dat)*	Eso:
There Is: *(Der Is)*	Hay:
Think: *(Sink)*	Pensar:
Tire: *(Taier)*	Rueda:
Together: *(Tugeder)*	Juntos:
Traffic Light: *(Trafic Lait)*	Semáforo:
Travel: *(Travel)*	Viajar:
Trip: *(Trip)*	Viaje:
Typewriter: *(Taip Raiter)*	Máquina de Escribir:
Under: *(Ander)*	Debajo:
Vacation: *(Vakeishon)*	Vacación:
Very: *(Veri)*	Muy:
Walk: *(Wok)*	Caminar:
While: *(Wail)*	Rato:
Whistle: *(Wisol)*	Pito:
Wild: *(Waild)*	Salvaje:
Win: *(Wuin)*	Ganar:
Winter: *(Winter)*	Invierno:
Wish: *(Wish)*	Desear:
(A) Wish:	Deseo:
With: *(Wis)*	Con:
Wonderful: *(Wonderful)*	Maravilloso:
Wrong: *(Wrong)*	Equivocado:

Fiestas Importantes
Important Holidays
(Important Jolideis)

Día de Conmemoración de Veteranos de la Guerra:

*Memorial Day: (**Memorial Dei**)*

Día de Gracias: *Thanksgiving Day: (**Sansgivin Dei**)*

Día de la Independencia: *Independence Day: (**Independes Dei**)*

Día de la Raza: *Columbus Day: (**Colombus Dei**)*

Día de las Brujas: *Halloween: (**Jalowin**)*

Día de los Enamorados (San Valentino):

*Valentine's Day: (**Valentains Dei**)*

Día de los Presidentes: *President's Day: (**Presidents Dei**)*

Día del Trabajador: *Labor Day: (**Leibor Dei**)*

Navidad: *Christmas: (**Crismas**)*

Noche Buena: *New Year's Eve: (**Niu Yirs Iv**)*

Semana Santa: *Easter: (**Ister**)*

Important Holidays
(Important Jolideis)
Fiestas Importantes

Christmas: *(Crismas)*   Navidad:

Columbus Day: *(Colombus Dei)*   Día de la Raza:

Easter: *(Ister)*   Semana Santa:

Halloween: *(Jalowin)*   Día de las Brujas:

Independence Day: *(Independes Dei)*

      Día de la Independencia:

Labor Day: *(Leibor Dei)*   Día del Trabajador:

Memorial Day: *(Memorial Dei)*   Día de Conmemoración de

      Veteranos de la Guerra:

New Year's Eve: *(Niu Yirs Iv)*   Noche Buena:

President's Day: *(Presidents Dei)*

      Día de los Presidentes:

Thanksgiving Day: *(Sansgivin Dei)*

      Día de Gracias:

Valentine's Day: *(Valentains Dei)*

      Día de los Enamorados (San
      Valentino):

Index

Better 176
Biblioteca 59, 161
Bibs 107
Bicarbonato de soda 90
Bide 75
Bidet 77
Bien, gracias 122
Big 145
Bigote 133
Bills 176
Bird 17
Birthday 126
Bistec 89
Bite 145
Black 56
Blackberry 92
Bladder 137
Blanco 55
Blanket 69, 107
Bleed 145
Blender 83
Bless you (When you
    sneeze) 126
Blind 145
Blinds 69
Blood 137
Blood Clot 145
Blouse 73
Blow 176
Blue 56
Blusa 71
Boca 133
Body 137
Boil 153
Bolsa de Agua (caliente)
    140
Bolsa de Hielo 140
Bolsa Fría 140
Bolsas de aspiradora 36
Bolsas de basura 36
Bombero 165
Bomberos 49
Bombillo/Foco 59
Bone 137, 145
Bonita 122
Book 69
Book shelf 69
Book Store 163

Boot 73
Booties 107
Bordado 101
Borrar 97
Bota 71
Botella 79
Both 176
Botica/Gabinete de
    medicina 75
Botón 71, 91
Bottle 83, 107
Bottle warmer 107
Bowl 83
Boy 168
Boyfriend 168
Bra 73
Bracelet 73
Brain 136
Brasa 97
Brasar 151
Brass polish 38
Brazos 134
Bread 94
Breakfast 24, 111
Breakfast room 61
Breast 145
Breath 145
Brick 176
Brillo 36
Brillo Pads 38
Bring 176
Broccoli 92
Broche 71
Brocoli 87
Broil 99, 153
Broke 176
Broken 145
Bronchia 137
Bronquio 134
Broom 38, 64
Broth 94
Brother 168
Brown 56, 153
Bucket 64
Buen provecho 122
Buena suerte 122
Buenas noches 122
Buenas tardes 122

Bueno 109
Buenos días 122
Bufanda 71
Building 163
Bulletin Board 176
Bulto/Hinchazón/Golpe
    140
Bump 145
Bunk bed 107
Burn 146, 153
Burner 83
Buró/Mesa de noche 67
Bus 7
Bus Driver 168
Buscar 171
Business man 168
Busto 140
Busy 51
But 176
Butcher 168
Butler 168
Butter 94
Butter server 83
Buttocks/Butt 137
Button 73, 99
By 176
Caballo 16
Cabbage 92
Cabeza 133
Cabinet 83
Cachetada 140
Cachetes 133
Cachucha 71
Cada 171
Cadena/Collar 71
Caderas 134
Café 88
Café/Marrón/Carmelita
    55
Cafetera 79
Cage 17
Caída 140
Caja de arena 105
Caja de música 105
Cajero 165
Cake 94
Cake pan 83
Calabacita verde 87

Clean 99, 111, 146, 153
Cleaners 163
Cleanser (powder) 38
Clear 56
Clinic 146
Clínica 140
Clock 69
Cloro 36
Clorox, Bleach 38
Closet 59, 61, 67, 69
Closet de comidas 79
Clothes 69, 73
Clothes Basket 64
Clothes detergent 38
Cloudy 58
Cloves 95
Coágulo de Sangre 140
Coals 177
Coat 73
Cobija 105
Cobija Eléctrica 140
Coche/Carrola 105
Cochino/Cerdo 16
Cocina 59
Cocinar 97
Cocinar al Fuego Lento 151
Cocine 151
Coco 87
Cocodrillo/Caimán 16
Coconut 92
Codo 134
Coffee 93
Coffee creamer 83
Coffee filter 83
Coffee maker 83
Colador 79
Colar 151
Colcha/Cobija 67
Cold - Cool 58
Cold 99, 111, 146
Cold Pack 146
Coleccionar 171
Colegio/Escuela 161
Coliflor 88
Collect 177
College/University 163
Columpio 105
Comal/Budare 79

Comb 77
Come 177
Come here please 51
Come in, please 126
Comedor 59
Comerciante 165
Comfortable 177
Comida 89
Comiendo 49
Comino 90
Cómo? 110
Cómo estás? 122
Cómo se llama? 122
Cómo te sientes? 122
Cómoda 105
Cómoda/Repisa 67
Cómodo 172
Compañero(a) de clase 165
Complain 177
Compota 105
Compras 161
Compresas 140
Compresses 146
Comprimidor de basura 79
Comprometido 165
Con 172
Con amigo/a 49
Con Frecuencia 171
Condensed milk 94
Congelador/friser 79
Congratulations 126
Conocer 172
Conservar 151
Consomé 89
Constipation 146
Contracción 140
Contraction 146
Cook 99, 153
Cook book 83
Cookie 94
Cookie cutters 83
Cooking sheet 83
Cooking wine 95
Cool 99, 153, 177
Copas (de vino) 79
Corazón 134
Corbata 71

Cord 146
Cordón 140
Cordón Eléctrico 97
Corduroy 102
Corn 92
Corn popper 83
Corner 177
Corral 105
Correa/Cinturón/Cinto 71
Correo (Estación) 161
Correo 59
Corriente 97
Cortada 140
Cortar 151
Cortina 67
Cortina de baño 75
Costumbre 172
Costurera 165
Cotton 102
Cotton ball 77
Couch 66
Cough 146
Counter 83
Country 163
Cousin 168
Cover 146, 153
Crawl 104
Cream 77, 94, 107
Cream cheese 94
Crema 105
Crema 75, 89
Crema agria 89
Crema de maní 89
Crema para lustrar bronce 36
Crema para lustrar platería 36
Cremera 79
Creo que si 110
Criada 165
Crib 107
Crónico 140
Crutch 146
Cry 104
Cuaderno 67
Cuadro 65, 67
Cuál? 110
Cuándo? 110

Lunch box 107
Lunes 18, 57
Lungs 137
Luz 75, 98
Lying down 147
Macaroni 94
Macarrones 89
Machacar 151
Madre 166
Magazine rack 69
Mailbox 61
Mailman 169
Make-up 77
Maleta/Petaca 173
Mall 163
Malo 110
Man 169
Manager 169
Mañana 5, 57, 110
Manejar Bicicleta 103
Manicurist 169
Manicurista 166
Manos 134
Manteca 90
Mantel 80
Manteles individuales 80
Mantequilla 90
Mantequillera 80
Many times 112
Manzana 87
Mapeador/trapeador 37
Maquillaje 75
Máquina de Coser 173
Máquina de Escribir 173
Máquina de lavar ropa 63
Máquina para hacer
    palomitas 80
Maravilloso 173
Marble 178
Marcador 98
March 58
Mareado 142
Mareo 142
Margarina 90
Margarine 94
Marinar 152
Marinate 153
Mariscos 90

Mármol 173
Married 8
Martes 18
Martes 57
Marzo 58
Más 110
Más o menos 110, 123
Más Tarde 173
Masage 142
Mascota 41
Mash 153
Mason 169
Massage 147
May 58, 178
May I help you? 128
Maybe 8
Mayo 58
Mayonesa 90
Mayonnaise 95
Mayordomo 166
Me permite? 123
Me siento mal 123
Measles 148
Measuring cup 84
Measuring spoons 84
Meat tenderizer 84
Mecánico 166
Mechanic 169
Medias 72
Medias de nailon 72
Medicina 142, 148
Medicine chest 77
Medio/mediano 98
Medio/Mitad 173
Medium 100
Meet 178
Mejor 173
Melocotón 55, 87
Melón 87
Melt 154
Menopause 148
Menopausia 142
Menos 110
Menstruación 134
Mental 142, 148
Mentir 103
Merengada/batido 88
Merienda 90, 110

Mermelada 90
Mes 5
Mesa 65, 67, 80
Mesa de juego 65
Mesedora 106
Meser 174
Mesita de Cama 142
Mesonero/Mesero 166
Metal 101, 102
Mezclar 152
Mezclilla 101
Mi nombre es 123
Micro-ondas 80
Microwave oven 84
Middle name 8
Miedo 5
Miércoles 18, 57
Mil 54
Mildew cleaner 39
Milk 93
Million 54
Millón 54
Mine 8
Minute 57
Minuto 57
Mío 5
Mirar 174
Mirror 69, 77
Miscarriage 148
Mismo 5
Miss 169
Mix 154
Mixer 84
Mobil 106
Mobile 107
Molar 136
Molde de gelatina 80
Molde de hornear 81
Molde para pastel/torta
    81
Moldes de galletas 81
Mole 137
Moler 152
Molino 81
Monday 18, 57
Monja 166
Monk 169
Monkey 17

Mono/Chango 16	My way 8	No mucho 5
Montaña 162	Nabo 88	No muy bien 124
Month 8	Nada 110	No sé 5
Moon 178	Nada 5	Noche 57, 174
Mop 39, 64	Nadar 103	Nombre 5
Mora 87	Nail polish 77	Nombre segundo (Medio) 5
Morado 55	Nailon 101	Nombres 25
Mordida 142	Nalgas 134	Noodles 95
More 112	Name 8	Nose 136
More or less 112	Names 25	Not applicable 18
Morning 57	Nap time 24	Not much 8
Mostaza 90	Napkins 84	Not yet 113
Mostrador 81	Naranja 87	Notebook 69
Mother 169	Naríz 133	Nothing 8, 112
Mother-in-Law 169	Náusea 142	November 58
Motor 174, 178	Nausea 148	Novia 166
Mountain 164	Near 8	Noviembre 58
Mouse 17	Necesito trabajar 5	Novio 166
Mouth 136	Neck 136	Now 8, 112
Move 148	Necklace 73	Nublado 58
Mover 142	Negro 55	Nueces 90
Movie Theater 164	Neighbor 148, 169	Nuera 166
Mr. 169	Nevando 58	Nuestro 174
Mrs. 169	Never 112	Nueve 54
Much 112	Nevera/Refrigerador 81	Nuez mozcada 90
Muchas veces 110	Next day 112	Number 8
Mucho 5, 110	Nice to meet you 128	Número 5
Mueblería 162	Nieta 166	Nun 169
Muela 133	Nieto 166	Nunca 110
Muestra 174	Nieve 174	Nurse 169
Mujer 166	Night 57	Nutmeg 95
Muleta 142	Night gown 73	Nuts 95
Muñeca 106, 134	Night light 69	Nylon 102
Muscle 137	Night stand 69	O.K 8, 128
Músculo 134	Niña/Hembra 166	Object 148
Museo 162	Nine 54	Objeto 142
Museum 164	Niño/Varón 166	Obrero 166
Mushroom 93	Niños 166	Obscuro 55
Music box 107	Nipple 137	Ocho 54
Musician 169	Nivel 98	October 58
Músico 166	No 5, 8, 110, 112	Octubre 58
Muslo 134	No entiendo/comprendo	Ocupado 50
Must 178	50	Of course 8
Mustache 136	No está 49, 110	Off 100
Mustard 94, 95	No estoy segura 5	Office 52, 61, 164
Muy 174	No hablo inglés 50	Oficina 50, 59, 162
Muy caro 123	No lo sabía 5, 123	Often 178
My name is 128	No me gusta 5	Oídos 133

Oil 95
Oil cleaner for wood
    furniture 39
Oir 174
Ojos 133
Okei 124
Old 148
Olla 81
Olla de baño maría 81
Olla de vapor 81
Ombligo 134
On 100, 178
Once a month 18
One 54
One moment please 52
Onion 93
Onion flakes 95
Only 8
Operación 142
Operador(a) 166
Operadora 50
Operation/Surgery 148
Operator 52, 169
Orange 56, 92
Orégano 90
Oregano 96
Organos Sexuales 134
Orina 142
Ornament 66
Orzuelo 142
Oso 16
Other 25
Otoño 174
Otras cosas 25
Otro 5
Our 178
Out of town 52
Outside/out 112
Ovario 134
Ovary 137
Oveja 16
Oven 84
Oven cleaner 39
Overalls 108
Overdose 148
Overoles 106
Owner 169
Oxígeno 142

Oxygen 148
Paciente 142
Pacifier 108
Package 178
Padre 166
Pagos 174
Pail/bucket 39
Pain/Ache 148
Paint 104
Painter 169
Painting 66
Pair 178
País 162
Pajamas 73
Pájaro 16
Pala de recoger basura 37
Pale 148
Pálido 142
Palillo de dientes 81
Palsy 148
Pan 89
Pan tostado 89
Pana 101
Panadera 167
Pañalera 106
Pañales 106
Pancake 94
Panecillos 89
Paño de cocina 81
Panqueca 89
Pantaletas 72
Pantalón 72
Pantalón corto 72
Pantalón de mezclilla 72
Panties 73
Pantorilla 134
Pantry 85
Pants 73
Pantuflas/Sapatillas 72
Panty hose 73
Pañuelo 72
Papa 88
Papel tualet/sanitario 75
Paper towel 39
Paper towel 85
Paprika 96
Paquete 174
Par 174

Para la secadora
    (Suavizador) 37
Parálisis 142
Parar 98
Parasites 148
Parásitos 142
Pared 59
Park 164
Párpado 133
Parque 162
Parrilla 81
Parsley 96
Part time 8
Parte del tiempo 5
Parto 142
Party 164
Pasado 174
Pasaporte 174
Pasillo 59
Pasita 87
Pass 178
Passport 178
Pasta de dientes 75
Pastel/torta 89
Pastelería 162
Pastilla 142
Pastor 167
Patient 148
Patinar 174
Patio 59, 174
Pausa 98
Pause 100
Pavo 90
Pay Phone 164
Payments 179
Peach 56, 92
Peanut butter 95
Pear 92
Peas 93
Peca 134
Pecho 134, 142
Pedazo 174
Pedestal 65
Pedestal/Stand 66
Peel 154
Peeler 85
Pegajoso 174
Peine 75

Pelador 81
Pelar 152
Pelear 103
Peligro 50, 142
Pelo/Cabello 133
Pelota 174
Peluquería 162
Peluquero(a) 167
Pen 179
Pencil 179
Pensar 174
Pepino 88
Pepper 96
Pepper shaker 85
Pequeña 142
Pequeño 98
Pera 87
Perder 174
Perdón 50
Perdóneme 124
Perejil 91
Perfume/Cologne 77
Perfume/Colonia 75
Period/Menstruation 137
Permanent press 100
Pero 174
Perro 16
Persiana 67
Pesa 76
Pesado 98, 174
Pescado 90
Peso 142
Pesón 134
Pestaña 133
Pet 41
Pez 16
Pharmacy 164
Piano 65, 66
Picada 142
Picar 152
Pickle 95
Picture 66, 69
Pie 134
Piece 179
Piel 135, 142
Piernas 135
Pies 135
Pig 17

Pijamas 72
Pila/bateria 98
Pill 148
Pillow 69
Pillow case 69
Pilot 169
Piloto 167
Pimentón rojo 91
Pimienta 91
Pimientero 81
Pimple 148
Pin 73
Piña 87
Pinch 148
Pineapple 92
Pink 56
Pintar 103
Pintor 167
Pintura 65
Pintura de uñas 76
Pinzas 76
Piscina/Alberca 59
Piso 59
Piso de cerámica 59
Piso de madera 59
Piso de Plástico 59
Pitcher 85
Pito 174
Placemats 85
Plan 179
Plancha 63
Plancha para waffles 81
Planchado permanente 98
Planear 174
Plant 69
Planta/Mata 67
Plantas 76
Plants 77
Plastic 102
Plástico 101
Plátano/banana/guineo 87
Plate 85
Plateado 55
Plato 81
Plato de servir 81
Plato hondo 81
Play 104, 164
Play room 61

Playa 162
Playpen 108
Playtime 25
Please 8, 128
Plomero 167
Plug 100
Plum 92
Pluma 174
Plumber 169
Poco 5, 110
Poison 148
Police 52, 148
Policeman 170
Policía 50, 142, 167
Poliester 101
Poliester 102
Pollo 90
Polvo de hornear 91
Polvo para limpiar 37
Polvo/Talco 76
Polvorear 152
Polyester 102
Pool 61
Por 174
Por favor 5, 124
Por Fín 174
Por qué? 110
Porch 61
Pork 95
Porque 174
Port 164
Porta bebé 106
Portón 59
Post Office 164
Postre 174
Pot 85
Potato 93
Pour 154
Powder 77
Power 100
Practicar 174
Practice 179
Pray 179
Precio 174
Pregnant 148
Pregunta 174
Prender 98
Prensa de ajo 81
Preparar 152, 174

Sala de familia 60
Sala de juegos 60
Sala de visitas 60
Salad 95
Salad bowl 85
Salad Dressing 95
Salero 81
Salesperson 170
Salpullido 106
Salpullido/Erupción de la
  piel 143
Salsa 90
Salsa inglesa 91
Salsa japonesa 91
Salsa para ensalada 90
Salsera 81
Salt 96
Salt shaker 85
Salud (estornudo) 124
Salud 143
Saludable 143
Salvaje 175
Salvavidas 106
Same 8
Sample 179
Sand box 108
Sandal 74
Sandalia 72
Sangrar 143
Sangre 135
Sarampión 143
Sartén 81
Satén 101
Satin 102
Saturday 18, 57
Sauce 95
Sauté 154
Say 179
Scale 77
Scar 148
Scared of 8
Scarf 74
School 164
Scissors 77
Scour/Scrape 179
Scrape 148
Scream 104
Scrub brush 39

Se ve bien 124
Seafood 95
Seamstress 170
Season 154
Seat 179
Seat Belt 179
Secadora 63
Secadora de madera 63
Secadora de pelo 76
Secar 152
Seco 58, 98
Second 57
Secretaria 167
Secretary 170
Seda 101
See you later 128
Segundo 57
Seguro 5
Seis 54
Semáforo 175
Semana 57
Send 179
Send my regards 128
Señor 167
Señora 167
Señorita 167
Sentir 143
Separado 6
Separated 8
September 58
Septiembre 58
Serve 154
Servilletas 81
Serving dish 85
Serving fork 85
Serving spoon 85
Servir 152
Seven 54
Sewing Machine 179
Sexual Organs 137
Shake 93, 154
Shampoo 78
Shampú 76
Shampú de bebé 106
Shaver 78
She 9
Sheep 17
Sheets 70

Shelf 70
Ship/Boat 164
Shirt 74
Shoe 74
Shoe rack 70
Shoe Repair Man 170
Shopping 52, 164
Short 112
Shorts 74
Shot 148
Shoulder pads 74
Shoulders 138
Shower 78
Shower curtain 78
Si 6, 110
Si me gusta 6
Sick 52, 128, 148
Siéntese aquí 124
Siesta 24
Siete 54
Signature 9
Silk 102
Silla 65
Silla 68, 76, 81
Silla de carro 106
Silla de comer 106
Silla de entrenar 106
Silla de Ruedas 143
Silver 56
Silver polish 39
Simmer 154
Sing 104
Singer 170
Single 9
Sink 64, 78, 85
Síntomas 143
Sister 170
Sit here 128
Six 54
Size 9
Skate 179
Skillet 85
Skim milk 93
Skin 138, 148
Skinny 112
Skirt 74
Slap 149
Sleep 104

Sleep well 128
Sleeper 108
Sleeping 52
Sleepy 179
Slice 154
Slide 108
Slip 74
Slippers 74
Slow 100
Slow please 52
Small 100, 149
Snack 95, 112
Snake 17, 149
Snow 179
Snowing 58
So so 128
Soak 100, 154
Soap 39, 78, 108
Soap dish 78
Soaps 64
Sobredosis 143
Socks 74
Sofá 65
Sofrito/Sofreir 152
Soft drink 93
Soft hair brush 108
Soil 100
Sol 175
Sólo 124
Sólo/solamente 6
Soltero 6
Sombrero 72
Sombrilla/Paraguas 72
Someone 179
Sometimes 179
Son 170
Son-in-Law 170
Soon 9
Sopa 88
Sopera/cucharón 81
Soplar 175
Sordo 143
Sostén/Brasier 72
Soup 93
Soup/cereal bowl 85
Sour 179
Sour cream 95
Soy sauce 96

Soya 91
Spaghetti 95
Spatula 85
Speed 100
Spell please 52
Spices 95
Spinach 93
Sponge 39, 64
Spoon (Tablespoon) 85
Spoon (Teaspoon) 85
Spot cleaner 39
Sprain 149
Spray cleaner for carpets
    39
Spread 154
Spring 179
Sprinkle 179
Squirrel 17
Stamp 179
Standard 9
Star 179
Starch 39
Start 100, 112
State 9
Station 164
Statue 66
Steak 95
Steal 180
Steam 100
Steamer 85
Step 62
Steps/Stair 62
Stereo 70
Sterile 149
Sterilizer 108
Stew 154
Sticky 180
Sting 149
Stir 154
Stomach 138
Stool 85, 149
Stop 100
Store 164
Stove 85
Strain 154
Strainer 85
Strawberry 92
Street 9, 164

Stroller 108
Student 170
Study 104
Stuffed 154
Sty 149
Subir 175
Such 180
Sucio 110
Sudor 143
Suede 102
Suegra 167
Suegro 167
Sueter/Chamarra 72
Suficiente 6
Sugar 96
Sugar bowl 85
Suit 74
Suitcase 180
Sujeta/Agarra 175
Summer 180
Sun 180
Sunday 18, 57
Supermercado 162
Support 149
Sure 9
Suyo 6
Swallow 149
Swear 180
Sweat 149
Sweater 74
Sweet 180
Sweet potato 93
Swim 104
Swing 108, 180
Swollen 149
Symptoms 149
Syrup 149
T-shirt 74
T.V. 66, 70
Tabla de planchar 63
Tabla para cortar 81
Table 70, 85
Table leaves 85
Table pad 85
Table/Coffee table 66
Tablecloth 85
Taburete/Banquillo 81
Take 149

Take Off 180
Tal 175
Tal vez 6
Talco de bebé 106
Talk 104, 112
Talla 6
También 175
Tampoco 175
Tapete 65, 76
Tarde 57
Tarea 24
Taxi Driver 170
Taxista 167
Taza 81, 98
Taza de medir 81
Tazón 81
Té 88
Te quiero 124
Tea 93
Tea kettle 85
Teacher 170
Tears 136
Teatro 162
Techo 60
Teeth 136
Tejidos 101
Teléfono 41, 68
Teléfono Público 162
Telephone 41, 70
Televisión 65, 68
Temperatura 143
Temperatura 58, 98
Temperature 58, 100, 149
Temporal/Temporario 6
Temporary 9
Ten 54
Tenazas 82
Tendón 135
Tendon 138
Tenedor 82
Tenedor de servir 82
Tener Sueño 175
Tenga un buen día 124
Tengo 6
Terciopelo 101
Teriyaki sauce 96
Terminar 110, 175

Termo 82
Termómetro 143
Terrace 62
Terraza 60
Tetera 82
Tetero/biberón/pacha/bo tella 106
Thank you 9, 128
That 180
The (Feminine) 112
The (Masculine) 112
The alarm 52
Theater 164
Theirs 9
There 112
There Is 180
Thermometer 149
Thermos 85
Thigh 138
Think 180
Thousand 54
Three 54
Throat 136
Thumb 138
Thursday 18, 57
Tía 167
Tibio 110
Tibio 98
Tie 74, 149
Tiempo completo 6
Tiempo/hora 98
Tienda 162
Tiene calor? 125
Tiene frío? 125
Tiene Usted? 110
Tierra 98, 175
Tiger 17
Tigre 16
Tijeras 76
Tile floor 62
Time 100
Time for snacks 24
Timer 85
Tin 86
Tina/Bañera 76
Tintorería/Lavandería 162
Tío 167

Tira pañales/Dispensa de pañales 106
Tire 180
To Pull 149
Toalla 76, 106
Toalla de papel 37
Toallas 37
Toallas de papel 82
Toallas mojadas 106
Toallera 76
Toast 94, 100, 154
Toaster 86
Tobillo 135
Tobo/Cubeta 63
Tobogán 106
Tocador 68
Tocador/Peinadora 76
Tocineta 90
Todavía no 110
Today 9, 112
Todo 110
Toenails 138
Toes 138
Together 180
Toilet 78
Toilet brush 39
Toilet paper 78
Toilet paper holder 78
Tomar 143
Tomate 88
Tomato 93
Tomorrow 112
Tomorrow 9
Tongs 86
Tongue 136
Tono 98
Tonsils 149
Tooth 136
Tooth brush 78
Tooth paste 78
Tooth pick 86
Torcedura 143
Toronja 87
Tortuga 16
Tos 143
Tostadora 82
Tostar 152
Tostar 98

HODGE
PRINTING COMPANY
11416 NEWKIRK ST.   DALLAS, TEXAS 75229